Destruction of Bialystok (Białystok, Poland)

Translation of
Khurbn Bialystok

Author: Srolke Kot

Originally published in Buenos Aires, 1947

A Publication of JewishGen, Inc.
Edmond J. Safra Plaza, 36 Battery Place, New York, NY 10280
646.494.5972 | info@JewishGen.org | www.jewishgen.org

Destruction of Bialystok (Białystok, Poland)
Translation of *Khurbn Bialystok*

Copyright © 2023 by JewishGen, Inc. All rights reserved.
First Printing: September 2023, Elul 5783

Author: Srolke Kot
Project Coordinator: Susan Kingsley Pasquariella
Translated by: Beate Schützmann-Krebs
Extraction of English text: Donni Magid
Cover Design: Irv Osterer
Layout: Jonathan Wind

Printed in the United States of America by Lightning Source, Inc.

Library of Congress Control Number (LCCN): 2023942702

ISBN: 978-1-954176-80-5 (hard cover: 118 pages, alk. paper)

About JewishGen.org

JewishGen, an affiliate of the Museum of Jewish Heritage - A Living Memorial to the Holocaust, serves as the global home for Jewish genealogy.

Featuring unparalleled access to 30+ million records, it offers unique search tools, along with opportunities for researchers to connect with others who share similar interests. Award winning resources such as the Family Finder, Discussion Groups, and ViewMate, are relied upon by thousands each day.

In addition, JewishGen's extensive informational, educational and historical offerings, such as the Jewish Communities Database, Yizkor Book translations, InfoFiles, Family Tree of the Jewish People, and KehilaLinks, provide critical insights, first-hand accounts, and context about Jewish communal and familial life throughout the world.

Offered as a free resource, JewishGen.org has facilitated thousands of family connections and success stories, and is currently engaged in an intensive expansion effort that will bring many more records, tools, and resources to its collections.

Please visit https://www.jewishgen.org/ to learn more.

Executive Director: Avraham Groll

About JewishGen Press

JewishGen Press (formerly the Yizkor Books-in-Print Project) is the publishing division of JewishGen.org, and provides a venue for the publication of non-fiction books pertaining to Jewish genealogy, history, culture, and heritage.

In addition to the Yizkor Book category, publications in the Other Non-Fiction category include Shoah memoirs and research, genealogical research, collections of genealogical and historical materials, biographies, diaries and letters, studies of Jewish experience and cultural life in the past, academic theses, and other books of interest to the Jewish community.

Please visit https://www.jewishgen.org/Yizkor/ybip.html to learn more.

Director of JewishGen Press: Joel Alpert
Managing Editor - Jessica Feinstein
Publications Manager - Susan Rosin

Notes to the Reader

The original book can be seen online at the Yiddish Book Center website:

https://www.yiddishbookcenter.org/collections/yiddish-books/spb-nybc209740/kot-srolke-khurbn-byalistok

Beate Schützmann-Krebs original work can be seen at: https://www.jewishbialystok.pl/Memorial-book-Khurbn-Bialystok,-written-by-Jewish-partisan-Srolke-Kot,-translated-into-English,5353,8526

A list of all books available from JewishGen Press along with prices is available at:
https://www.jewishgen.org/Yizkor/ybip.html

Translator's Foreword to
"Destruction of Bialystok"

Srolke Kot describes his experiences in Bialystok during the Shoah in simple but incredibly moving words. He recalls, in vivid detail, how he, along with other Jews and Russians, fought as partisans in the forests until liberation by the Red Army.

Miraculously, he survived unimaginably hostile and life-threatening conditions, and he appeals to us to be vigilant and to resist with all means against any inhuman fascist system.
The key to survival, according to Kot, was active and vigorous resistance.

I sincerely thank my friends, Susan Kingsley Pasquariella, Tomek Wisniewski, Joanna Czaban and Miroslaw Reczko for their great support and the author's family for their friendly cooperation.

Special thanks to JewishGen for making this book possible.

Beate Schützmann-Krebs
July 2023
Germany

Geopolitical Information

Białystok, Poland is located at 53°08' N 23°09' E and 109 miles NE of Warszaw

	Town	District	Province	Country
Before WWI (c. 1900):	Belostok	Białystok	Grodno	Russian Empire
Between the wars:	Białystok	Białystok	Białystok	Poland
After WWII (c. 1950):	Białystok			Poland
Today (c. 2000):	Białystok			Poland

Alternate Names for the Town:

Białystok [Pol], Byalistok [Yid], Belostok [Rus], Belastok [Bel], Balstogė [Lith], Bjalistoka [Latv], Bialistok, Bielastok

Nearby Jewish Communities:

Wasilków 5 miles NNE

Choroszcz 7 miles W

Supraśl 10 miles NE

Zabłudów 12 miles SE

Suraż 15 miles SSW

Łapy 16 miles SW

Tykocin 16 miles WNW

Knyszyn 16 miles NW

Jasionówka 18 miles NNW

Michałowo 20 miles ESE

Zawady 21 miles W

Narew 21 miles SE

Sokoły 21 miles WSW

Gródek 22 miles E

Korycin 22 miles N

Janów Sokolski 23 miles N

Trzcianne 24 miles NW

Sokółka 24 miles NE

Bielsk Podlaski 25 miles S

Krynki 28 miles ENE

Goniądz 29 miles NW

Rutki 30 miles W

Wysokie Mazowieckie 30 miles WSW

Brańsk 30 miles SSW

Jewish Population: 47,783 (in 1895), 44,940 (in 1939)

Map of Poland showing the location of **Białystok**

Destruction of Bialystok
(Białystok, Poland)

53°08' / 23°09'

Translation of *Khurbn Bialystok*

Author: Srolke Kot

Buenos Aires, 1947

Acknowledgments

Project Coordinator:

Susan Kingsley Pasquariella

Translator:

Beate Schützmann-Krebs

**Our sincere appreciation to Susan Kingsley Pasquariella and
Beate Schützmann-Krebs, for their permission to put this
Material on the JewishGen web site.**

**We wish to thank Donni Magid for extracting the English translation,
enabling this online presentation.**

This is a translation of: *Khurbn Bialystok*
Bialystok and its Destruction,
Author: Srolke Kot. Published by a group of friends, Buenos Aires, 1947

סראלסקע סאס

כורבן ביאַליסטאָק

אָלייסאַנעסאַמען פֿון
אַ נריאַק פֿרייגוש
בוענאָס איירעס 1947

KHURBN BYALISTOK

Srolke Kot

•

NATIONAL YIDDISH BOOK CENTER

AMHERST, MASSACHUSETTS

[Cover of the original book, courtesy of Dr. Tomek Wisniewski]

Page 3

Khurbn Bialystok
[Destruction of Bialystok]
Srolke Kot

Translation from Yiddish to English: Beate Schützmann-Krebs

Published by a group of friends, Buenos Aires, 1947

Page 7

Bialystok and its Destruction

By publishing the book "Khurbn Bialystok" the committee fulfills not only a social obligation to the city of Bialystok, which heroically defended itself against the enemy of the Jewish people and whose sons maintained courage and fighting spirit under the most difficult conditions. Those sons were characterized by such deep human solidarity with the fellow sufferer and acted heroically in the unequal struggle in the ghetto when the ghetto was surrounded.

Bialystok — this was not a name of a city in the usual sense of the word. Bialystok was a great cultural center, which not only provided the Jewish world with intelligence, but also, through the mass of its workers, held the finest traditions of the struggle for freedom and justice. Moreover, the martyred city of Bialystok, tormented and trampled by the German murderers, resisted in such conditions that we cannot even imagine, rose to the ghetto uprising and defended the soil of the Jewish people, unaffected by the fact that the struggle was doomed from the outset to certain death.

The author of the book "Khurbn Bialystok", Srolke Kot, who endured the hardships of the ghetto and later bore the struggle in the forest on his own shoulders, is himself a sufferer, a witness and accuser against the perpetrators of the cruel crime. It was not his intention to write a literary work, but to bring to light the naked truth about what happened; and that about which he could not write is felt by the reader,

Page 8

in the humble, simple words of the partisan "Kot", a soldier of the Jewish people.

With the publication of this book we provide another document to the history of our martyrdom, to the history of heroic Bialystok, whose courage and example serves as a light pillar for future generations.

Buenos Aires, April 1947,
the editors

Page 9

The Outbreak of the War

Even a week before the outbreak of the war, the tense situation was not felt in Bialystok. Living conditions were normal; everyone went to work. A part of men of all ages had left with the Red Army. Those who stayed in the city had a pleasant time. The city was flourishing in the Soviet way: There were big stores, places that provided diversion and entertainment, and other things. People enjoyed themselves and would never have believed that Bialystok would be taken by the Germans in just a week.

I still remember the last Shabbat. I go to a restaurant with my friends for a glass of wine, and then as usual I go for a walk with them in the forest. There we lingered until one o'clock in the morning, and later, when I get home, Mom opens the door for me and says:

"Tomorrow you have to get up and go to work!"

I get undressed and go to sleep, but I can't fall really asleep yet. That's when I'm jolted awake by a loud impact of a bomb that has fallen nearby. I get dressed, run out into the street and see a few people asking each other:

"What happened?"

The answer, "probably maneuvers!"

So people can go back to sleep; no one expects that there is already war.

We stop for a bit and see a bandaged person running, shouting: "A bomb has fallen! There are dead people there! It's war!" We don't believe it. I run to check it out. I reach the second street on Nayvelt [New World, Nowy Świat]. The small Pyotrokovski Street

Page 10

is already half in ruins.

I run into the collapsed houses and step on a naked woman, whom I can barely recognize as a human being because she is lying between a pile of bricks and is covered with dust.

People are running with shovels to dig out the buried people in several houses. Wounded people can be seen. The window panes of all the buildings on the street are cracked. Homeless people drag themselves desperately with their luggage to a garden on Nayvelt [Nowy Świat]. With their belongings, sleepy, confused and nervous, they are sitting in the garden.

German planes are already circling, every few minutes people run to the bushes to hide there. At dawn, a bomb had already hit the garrison by the forest, killing many Red Army soldiers who had been sleeping there unsuspectingly. In the civilian houses in the area there are many victims. Leaflets are already being distributed to register for military service at the Voyenkomat (1).

One goes there to register, but meets no one, everything is closed. Party members with rifles keep order in the street. The war can already be felt now.

Molotov's speech is posted outside, in which he reports that the Germans have attacked us barbarically and we must defend ourselves. It is already clear to everyone that this is an illegal invasion by Hitler's Germany. The youth and the elders decide to leave with the Red Army.

Trucks from organizations and factories take the workers who want to go deeper into the Soviet Union.

The mood is depressed. One asks the other, what will happen?

The Red Army is leaving us! During the one-week German occupation in 1939, the Jews of Bialystok had already felt what Hitler's Germany meant. Even then, Jews from the municipal office had been murdered in a bestial manner in the courtyard, and those who had been mortally wounded had been buried while still alive. During this week,

---

(1)   *author's note: military command*

Page 11

they had also looted the Jewish stores in the evenings during closing time. Therefore, everyone walks around with questioning looks and bowed heads.

We Flee from the Nazis

I run to the train station. The trains are crowded with women and children. Everyone is leaving to escape and not to see the Germans. I come home and suggest to my parents to leave; my brothers are not at home. As I sit and think, tears come to my eyes. As a returnee from the "Polish-German war," I know what war means.

Then my younger brother, Nyome, comes in. He sees me sitting there depressed and says, "You've already been to war, and you're still sitting there in such a daze? Come on, let's escape deeper into the Soviet Union!" I answer him, "Yes, take my bicycle and go! I will be able to walk better than you, because you are weaker!" Nyome takes my bicycle and says goodbye to everyone. We have not seen him again.

My second brother, Beybe (Leybl) has left from a factory in a truck. I say goodbye at home and assure [them]: "I have returned from the last war, so this time we will also meet again!" I receive a bicycle and together with other thousands of young people and elders, with all who can muster the strength, I ride deeper into the Soviet Union to help defeat Hitler's Germany.

On the Highway, we are going from Volokovysk towards Minsk, deeper and deeper into Russia. The further we go, the more we meet thousands of men, with women and children, moving along. A part is already on the way back, with the statement that it is impossible to go on, because the highway is bombed and there are already many fatalities there. We are not deterred by this. We go on walking, already sensing the German planes, incoming low, literally as low as man's height, firing their machine guns into the civilian population.

Page 12

Where people are hiding, in the trenches and in the rye field, there are dead and wounded. After such a shelling, a comrade comes running to me and shouts, "My wife and child are lying in the field; dead!"

A woman lies in a ditch. A child of one and a half years crawls on her and screams crying: "Mama!". From the cornfield a crying voice yells, "Tovorishtshi spasaytye!" ("Save me, comrades!")

It tears the heart. We approach a beautiful young girl lying there with a leg shot.

She asks to be taken to the hospital. Lightly wounded men limp and drag themselves forward. Farmers' carts carry nearly unconscious, wounded people. This is how the German air fleet accompanied us on all highways, leaving such pictures after each bombing.

We decide to continue on side roads, because it is no longer possible to go on the highway. But even there the planes do not let us live. They bomb us so violently that during a bombardment in the forest the whole earth shakes under us lying on the ground.

We continue on the highway again.

Dead bodies are lying everywhere. A 30-year-old boy is lying there with a bullet through his leg, he is bleeding. He begs me to save him. But no one comes, everyone just walks forward absent-minded. On the highway, overturned tanks and trucks block the way, everything stops and jams for miles until the way is cleared.

The Red Army soldiers want to get to Minsk as soon as possible in order to resist there. The Red Army men are completely absorbed by this thought. On the highway there are many coats, the best skins, new boots. Nobody pays attention to them. All of them have only one goal; to make their way as quickly as possible to the Soviet Union and help with the resistance there.

We go through Volkovysk. The city is on fire. The Red Army soldiers are still fighting in the city. We hear the shots and impacts. That's all that can be heard. The night falls. We ask the Red Army men to take us on their trucks; we are going with them together, now.

Suddenly—

Page 13

from the nearby houses on the highway they shoot at us! The trucks stop, everyone gets off them and the Red Army soldiers position themselves to fight. We also receive rifles. We see searchlights circling around us, we are surrounded. We open fire and manage to break through and continue, but the way is blocked by burned trucks, tanks and all kinds of automatic weapons.

Everyone, civilians and military, continues to walk. We no longer pay attention to the dead and wounded. We meet familiar comrades, a greeting, a question, an answer, and we walk on. We leave the highway and walk again on side paths. We take edibles from the dropped packets lying on the highway. I take some cookies and canned food. Meanwhile, I meet two Russians from Gomel who last worked in Bialystok. We become friends and walk together, but the bombings do not allow us any rest. We are tired from all that and sit down to eat something.

The Russians are unpacking schnapps. One Russian does not sit down but is looking for something. I ask him, "What are you looking for, why don't you sit down to eat?" He answers me that in 1928 he was exactly at this place and also drank schnapps. He left a glass behind at that time, which he is now looking for, because it is difficult to drink from a bottle with four people.

But he can't remember exactly the shrub, it's been too long, he has forgotten the external features...we laugh, sit down, drink from the bottle and eat canned food.

On the Way to Slonim

After dinner we move on. Night falls. We head for the highway; it is quieter at night. The highway is continuously packed and clogged with military of all formations. We are taken on a vehicle. We drive. The forests of the area are still burning from the bombardments during the day and from the battles we fought against the enemy incursions of the Germans above us.

We drive a whole night in the direction of Slonim on different ways. As soon as it gets lighter near a village, they open

Page 14

Bialystok of Old

Bazarna [Market] Street, the town clock and the little stores, the Polish Church and the way to the German Street

The central Vashlikover [Wasilkow] Street (Mitskevitsh)

Page 15

The Devastated Bialystok

The old "Hegdesh" [asylum for poor and sick Jews] on Sisurazer [Suraska] Street; in the Moyshev-Skeynim [home for the elderly], the people's kitchen and the reading room.

Once, this was the "Tank Fisher Yard", where you could walk through from the fish market to Zurazer [Suraska] Street.

*[**translator's note**: I assume a spelling mistake here, as the same place is called "Tanchum the Fisher's" fish market in the "Bialystok Photo Album," which makes more sense. According to the historian Dr. Tomek Wisniewski, the square in question can be found on old maps under the name "Rybny Rynek".]*

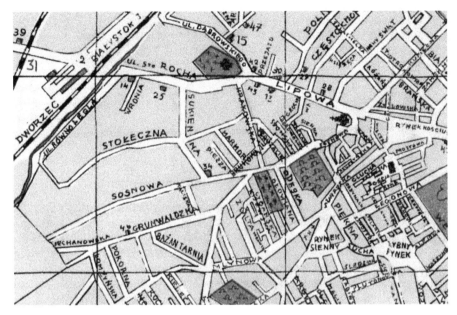

photo courtesy of Dr. Tomek Wisniewski

Page 16

fire on us. The bullets fly in the direction of the trucks on which we ride. We turn into the nearby forest. But there a German outpost is positioned, blocking our way. As soon as we regroup in the forest, he gives a signal and a hail of bombs pours out of the planes. The forest is already on fire. We are positioning ourselves for battle. Tired of the road and the battle, I say to my comrade, "I'm going to sleep; let the bullet or the bomb hit me while I'm sleeping!" And I show him the place where I am going to sleep.

When I get up at dawn, I find burned trucks in the forest; civilians and many soldiers are camped there. I look around - none of my acquaintances is among them, I am left alone. I walk around searching and see groups of people camped there, but I don't know anyone. A captain of the Red Army and several soldiers laager there, I ask him to take me to the front. He replies:

"Bring a compass and we will go together!"

I run to look for a compass, but no one has one. I continue searching in the forest, no acquaintances here.

In between, I hear a woman's voice: "Water!"

I look and see a woman from Bialystok lying, half fainted, also going along with the Red Army. I hook her under and lead her to just a little water in a puddle. She drinks her fill and thanks me for saving her life. She asks to be allowed to walk with me. Her strength is fading.

I see that everything is desperate here, you have to go on. But the forest is surrounded by Germans, you can't get out. In the distance I see railroad tracks. I take a chance and slowly slide on my stomach to the rails, maybe it is possible to break out of the encirclement. As I approach, I see a bombed, overturned train. On the side several dead men and women and on a wagon lie some bicycles.

I take a bicycle and go to a village to find out where I am. As I enter the village, a farmer's wife comes to meet me. The first thing I do is ask her for food. She gives me a jug of sour milk, which I drink in one go, and ask her where I am.

Page 17

She answers that there are already Germans in the area and that we are 5 kilometers away from Slonim. My heart sinks. From a hill I see in the distance people walking in black clothes and I realize that they are Germans. I decide to walk through forests and fields to avoid them and make my way deeper into the Soviet Union. When I have left the village and walked 100 meters, I hear from a bush: "Stoy! [Stop]!" I look around and see a major from the Red Army and two soldiers hiding there. They ask me what I did in the village and I tell them. They check my documents and see that my document says "Yeyrev" (Jew); they are sure that I am not a spy and release me.

I ask them for the way to the Soviet Union, they show it to me. But I see that it is impossible to go further. Germans are lying in the bushes and shooting from ambush. As I stand there completely alone and desperate, I think about what to do now. I put the bicycle aside and walk slowly on. There I meet two Jews from Slonim. They suggest I go with them to Slonim.

I explain to them that the Germans are already in Slonim and they will shoot us as Jews; we had better go through forests and fields to the Soviet Union. They talk at me for a long time and try to convince me that the Germans are not doing anything there, one can go into the city. For lack of food and other things I have no other way out and have to go with them to Slonim, which is already occupied by the Germans.

My First Encounter with the Germans

While walking with them, I still try to convince them to make their way to the Soviet Union, but it is not possible. After a few kilometers you can already see Slonim and the Germans walking around there. It becomes melancholy and depressed. A hot day, the sun is burning and all thirsts [for water]. The fields are green, but instead of grain there are burnt trucks

Page 18

and tanks. I throw away the coat I am carrying and go to the city. From afar we hear, "Halt! Hände hoch!" ["Stop! Hands up!"] I see shiny revolvers being drawn and pointed at us. "Stehen bleiben!" ["Freeze!"] We stop; looking over wordlessly. I sense death. We are searched and led to a yard with our hands raised. There they ask us immediately: "Jews? They're about to be shot!" and laugh sadistically. We do not answer. "Jews?" they shout at us again. The other two say—Jews. I know what's coming and answer: Pole, and pretend that I don't understand German. Immediately the Jews are "taken care of". They are placed facing the wall and told that they are about to be shot. They plead, cry, that they should be allowed to live. They tremble with fear all over their bodies. The Germans discuss how they will murder the Jews. I continue to pretend that I don't understand German. They call in an interpreter. I speak in Polish and the interpreter translates into German. They talk for a long time. The first thing they do is beat me until I bleed and say that they will also shoot me. I remain completely indifferent. After all, I have prepared myself for this and I already regret that I let them talk to me. Such beautiful weather, such a world, I haven't been able to enjoy it at all, and soon it will all be over....

While I remain in mortal fear and brooding for a while, the German begins to inflict various sadistic taunts and blows on me once again. After that he tells me to leave and shows me the direction. Slowly, as if not surprised by this, I begin to walk and look around to the rear to see if there is no shooting, because usually they order to walk and then shoot from behind. After walking two hundred meters on a long road in the direction of Slonim, I hear a shot. Not far from me falls a Red Army soldier who manages to still shout "Voda!" ["Water!"]. I continue walking towards the city, take out my Soviet passport and my military book and tear it up so that I can continue walking

Page 19

as a Pole without documents. I did not suspect that from behind I was still being watched by the German who ordered me to leave. When he sees that I am tearing something, he yells from afar "Stop! Freeze!" I stop. He runs to me with his shiny revolver and asks me what I tore. I continue to pretend I don't understand him. He hits me again and takes me to a house where many civilians are sitting. He brings me to an officer and tells him everything that happened. The officer asks me what I tore up. I pretend not to understand. He orders me to sit apart and tells the soldier to go away. I am a little relieved, maybe with time he will forget what he was going to ask me. While sitting in the house, I see a Red Army soldier being brought in. The officer orders him to be shot. A German leads him away. A shot is heard, then another.... When he returns, the German laughingly reports how he shot him. The officer pats the German on the back with satisfaction. In the courtyard other civilians are tormented, they are led away and shot without questioning them. I realize the misery I am in.

When night falls, a woman who knows many languages goes around and interrogates those who have survived. She examines the hands of each one to see if he is a worker. Some she releases, others she lets lead away, which means their death. She comes to me and questions me. I answer in Polish that I am coming from work, was sent to Russia and am on my way home from Minsk to Bialystok. She looks at my hands, they are dirty, all this time they were not washed. She determines that I am telling the truth and lets me go to Slonim that night.

It is dark. I don't know where to go. Then I see Jewish writing on a door. I go into the corridor, knock on the door and ask to be let in. From the other side of the door I am asked, "Do you have a document?" I answer, "no." They are afraid to let me in. I go to sleep in the corridor, at the foot of the door, my head rests on my hand. At dawn, a Jew wakes me up and questions me. They are

Page 20

all scared, they are afraid to let anyone in without a passport. They give me food. All day long, the neighbors hide in the attic. Through the cracks we see how Jews who are picked up on the street are beaten until they faint. Screams from Germans and pleading voices from defenseless Jews. This is the situation of Slonim in the first days under the Germans. The town has 60 percent Jews. I sleep in the house for a few days, they bring me a bed. It is decreed that until 30 years Jews must sleep in the Synagogue. When some of them are taken out, some come wounded by blows and some do not come back at all. I learn that one can get "travel papers" to go home and decide to turn back to Bialystok. The German is everywhere anyway.

I Return to Bialystok

I arrive at the municipal office, the courtyard there is full of people. Papers are handed out at tables and people enter that they are on their way home. The Germans dump the leftovers on the ground after the meal they received from nuns. Like wild animals, we throw ourselves on the ground and eat them, mixed with sand. I have to stand and wait for two days and receive a paper. People faint from hunger. A lad from Bialystok has gone blind after not being given food for 7 days. After he is given some food, he comes to. Human corpses with already rotten limbs are brought to Slonim. They are covered with flowers and buried in large "fraternal graves". I go to see if perhaps among them is my traveling companion. But there is no face to be recognized. In masses Red Army soldiers are led from the battlefields and forests. Among them are wounded and weak who can hardly walk. They support each other. The mood is depressed. The Germans are even giving travel papers to Moscow (it seems that they have hurried a bit…).

Page 21

Under these conditions I leave Slonim together with several more Bialystokers.

On these hottest days of the year, without food, completely broken and depressed, we, one from Volkovisk and a comrade from Bialystok, Feyvl Yoskulka, decide to return to Bialystok on foot. The heat burns like fire. Hungry and thirsty we walk on the highway. Every two meters there are dead bodies not yet cleared away, broken and burned vehicles and tanks. Many groups of people go there, each of them somewhere else. The whole Highway is crowded with German military of different formations. When they see us pass, they shout from the line, "Jews!" Each of the Germans pulls himself up like a dog on a chain, pointing his hands to his neck, as if to strangle and shoot Jews. We walk depressed, thinking that every minute we are threatened with death by these wild animals. No, they are even worse than animals, because a satiated animal does no harm to anyone. People are stopped all the time. Some are shot, others are forced to bury the dead and then murdered as well, then people are let go. These are still "good Germans".

All along the way, the villages are burned, some completely and some partially; only chimneys remain and here and there a chicken or a wandering cat walks out, which has not yet forgotten where its home once used to be. We take food from the cellars where the farmers keep potatoes. We take a few raw potatoes, not many, because we don't have the strength to carry them, and go on. From a distance we see the Germans stopping a group of people, checking them, taking them away and shooting them on the side; for no reason, just because they are Jews; or else, if they have short-cropped hair, because they are Red Army soldiers. We hide and when the Germans have passed, we crawl out of our hiding place and go on. We see the Jews and Red Army men who have just been shot. One minute

Page 22

earlier they were alive and dreaming, now their parents are waiting in vain for a letter from their sons...

We manage 35 kilometers on this day. Night falls, it's approaching closing time. We drag ourselves to a few houses where Jews live. This is Zelve [Zelva]. Once a large shtetl with many Jews, now only a few wander around in fear. We go to sleep and at dawn continue on our way to Volkovisk. On the highway are driving trucks with prisoners. From the trucks we are asked: "Kuda nas vzyat?" ["Where are they taking us?"] (1) We are afraid to answer because the Germans might shoot us just for talking to prisoners. Red Army prisoners are led on foot, Germans pass them on bicycles and shoot any prisoner who cannot or barely walk and falls back a little. The Germans first give the prisoners a short break in the middle of the road, then order them to get back in line, and finally shoot into their group for no reason. Others, observing this, hide in the overturned trucks and tanks, but they are shot into. By the time we reach Bialystok, hardly a few of the tens of thousands of prisoners will remain...

We go to a village and ask for food. The farmers say that they have nothing, because so many people pass through and they have to give something to everyone. But here and there we get a piece of bread. They tell us that the Germans are killing all the Jews in the shtetlekh and in many shtetlekh the Poles are helping to do it. We go on and towards evening we arrive in Volkovisk, which is completely burned. The comrade from Volkovisk takes us to his parents, who live in the burned bathhouse, because there are no apartments left. His mother cooks some food on a brick in a piece of tin and asks us to sleep on the ground. In the morning we say goodbye to them and leave Volkovisk.

In Horodok we see in the distance the burnt sawmill. I inquire with the Khayot family, our acquaintances. They tell me that my brother Nyome was there and persuaded the youth, no one had

---

(1)   ***translator's note****: literally, "Where are they calling us?"*

Page 23

to flee with the Red Army. Beybe was also with them, already on the way back, with his hat shot through. Because of the rapid encirclement, no one had been able to make it to the

Soviet Union. I am only 40 kilometers short of Bialystok. I sleep through the night and then set off once again.

What the Germans Did Shortly after They Entered Bialystok

Four kilometers before Bialystok we can already see the church spire. We feel happier to finally be in the city after such a walk. Our feet are lifting with more courage and we are already going faster. When we turn from Varshavske [Warszawska] Street, we already see the burnt municipal office, a few civilians, but no Jews. The streets are full of German military. I hurry through the side streets to our house. Only two weeks "the German" is here, and already such a great destruction! The very next day, after the Germans entered the city, they surrounded the entire Synagogue courtyard and Suraska, Legyonova [Legonowa] and Pyaske [Piezza] Street all the way to the woods, with troops walking around with their sleeves rolled up, weapons in their hands and grenades in their belts. They entered the small Zalevne [Zalewna Street], Genshe [Gesia] and Pivne Street and other surrounding alleys, invaded all the houses where Jews live, drove the men out and filled the [Great] Synagogue with them, which they set on fire with the living Jews inside. About a thousand people perished. Jews they encountered in the streets were shot. Some of them they threw alive into the burning Synagogue; one German grabbed the head, another the legs, they took a momentum, and the Jew was already lying in the flames of the Synagogue, writhing in pain. Some in the Synagogue who did not want to be burned hanged themselves by their trouser belts. A Christian sneaked along

Page 24

and opened the side door of the Synagogue. Thirty Jews escaped outside and told what was happening inside. It was the "strozh" [janitor] of the Synagogue who had done this. But there were also people who even showed the Germans where Jews lived.

But that is not all. The Germans go into all the alleys around the Synagogue, throwing detonation grenades into the houses, shooting the women, and impaling the children on their bayonets in front of their mothers. Many Jews are shot as they try to crawl over fences to save themselves. This lasted for a whole day. All the small streets around the Synagogue burned. The atmosphere is mingled with gunshots and screams.

Exactly how many Jews perished is not known. Many are carrying charred or half-burned people who were brought out. The Jews in the other streets who were in hiding were not harmed, but each of them had a missing family member. Many of the rescued come out with only what they had on their bodies.

A few days later, the Germans went house to house in the remaining streets, pulled out the men, lined them up, and asked, "What are you, a worker or an intellectual worker?" The men didn't know what to answer. Should they say an 'intellectual worker'? That was no good, because as a 'scholar' you were [with them] a communist whom they would shoot. Should they say an 'ordinary worker'? Then you would clearly be a communist and would also be shot. They were at a loss. Everyone stated exactly what they were not, hoping to save themselves. But, it came to the same thing; whatever they said, they were arrested, led through the streets. They were ordered to sing Jewish songs and dance, with various tricks. We do not know where they were taken. They were immortalized under the name of Thursday because this happened on Thursday. The woman who lost her husband or son that day was now called

Page 25

"di Donershtike" [The Thursday's]. If one told that she was one of the "Thursday's", one knew what that meant.

Every day Jews were seized at work. It was considered the greatest luck if one came home from work and had not been beaten. There was no more talk of getting paid for the work. In some places one was given a bit of soup to eat for a whole day's work, and if there was anything left over, and if it happened that one was allowed to take something for the second time, one brought some of it home for one's wife and child. Many Jews from the Synagogue courtyard, who had only been able to save their bare skin, began to look for work in order to have something to eat.

But for the Germans, this is still nothing. On the second Shabbat, the streets are cordoned off and all men who went to work were arrested. In addition, they go from house to house and take out all the men, without distinction whether young or old. They are all driven to the "zawierzyniec", to the park in the forest, where the football field is. They are beaten and tortured in an inhuman way. Their screams can be heard far into the forest and in the city.

Before that time the "Judenrat" had already been formed [with its seat] in the house of the old people's home, Kupyetske [Kupiecka] Street 34. One runs to the Judenrat and asks to mediate so that the arrested Jews are released. The Judenrat sends principals to the then head of the city. The latter orders them to sign a document stating that the Russians, before leaving the city, had set fire to the Jewish quarter with the Great Synagogue. They, the Germans, had only extinguished the fire. At gunpoint, the rabbi, Dr. Roz[en]man, signs the document. But that's not all. "The Executioner" demands tributes of several kilos of silver and a few million rubles. Then, he announces, he will release the Jews. Having no other choice, the demand is published by the Judenrat. Women go about the city, crying and pleading: "They don't want gold, [only] silver and money, save our husbands and sons!"

Page 26

Rings, silver candlesticks and everything that can be given are brought to the Judenrat. On the door of the Judenrat there is a large poster: "All administrators of stores and institutions or directors of factories who still have 'government money' from the time of Soviet rule must bring it as a tribute to the Judenrat, otherwise they will be expelled from the Jewish community". Several days in a row, everything they have is brought in to save the people, even more is collected than "the German" asked for. They bring it in, and the answer is: "Tomorrow they will all be released!" But the Germans have already killed them, and until today one still waits for the "tomorrow". Later we learned that they were taken outside the city to the road between Vashilkove [Wasilków] and Pyetrashe [Pietrasze

Forest] and shot there. Not one of the 3000 Jews, young and old, has come back as of today. The women whose husbands and children were arrested on that Shabbat were immortalized with the name "Shabesdike" [The Shabbat's]. From our family, among the "Shabbat's" were the brother of Khlavne's wife, the brother of Genye and Khayim Velvel, the brother of Feyge Bayle. That's all I remember. I and Beybe managed to lie hidden in the attic that day and not get between them.

The First Partisan

In all the commotion of people standing next to the Judenrat, shocked, silent, looking at each other with questioning looks as to what to do, a comrade joins them, Epshteyn. He sticks a small note on the door of the Judenrat that one should not bring consecrated rings and silver candlesticks as contribution, because it will come to extermination anyway, unless one offers resistance. They read the little note, which is barely visible next to the big poster with the "Exclusion" and they say: " Resistance ". That's another blow, like the one people got when the Russians withdrew on all fronts, "how can we Jews offer

Page 27

resistance?"… Comrade Epshteyn later perished in the battle with the Germans, when he was with me as a partisan in the forest in 1943. He was Feygl's friend, the son of Khaye the Grober's [digger], who had a store in "Breml" [Bialystok street or quarter with many Jewish stores].

The new legal decisions against the Jews do not come to an end yet. Jews are forbidden to walk on the sidewalk, all Jews must walk on the pavement, near the gutter or in the gutter. The sidewalk is only for the Germans and other nations.... Very few Jews are on the streets; at work they are grabbed and beaten. The gathering point for all is at the Judenrat. The situation is

Nyome Kot, perished in detention camp

very bad. Those who put down a stash of food before the Russians left can eat; but those from the area around the Synagogue are victims of fire and have lost everything. They go around hungry and eat at acquaintances' or friends' houses. There are still a few good workplaces where you can get a little food for your work; at dawn thousands of Jews come

Page 28

to "Shteyn" (1) and "Batshnitse" [Bocznica]. But only a few hundred are taken, the others are beaten because they crowd. There is no bread at all. People trade with each other, one has flour and needs groats, the other has potatoes and needs milk for a small child. The person who arranges the barter also earns something for it.

When I came home from the walk, the first thing I had to do was lie down in bed. While walking I did not feel the pain in my feet. I had walked with impetuosity, but as soon as I crossed the threshold into our apartment, I could no longer take a step and had to lie down. At home I met my parents, Leyble and my sister. Nyome did not return from his walk. I learn from my comrade, who had gone home with him, that an old woman they met on the way had asked Nyome to help her carry a package of things. In the package of things Nyome took from her, she had put in a military shirt, many of which were lying on the highway. The Germans later stopped [the small group] and searched them. Based on the shirt, they mistook Nyome for a Red Army soldier who had changed clothes and took him [and the comrade] into custody. My comrade suggested that he escape, but Nyome was very exhausted, had swollen feet from marching and could not run away. Nyome stayed in the prison camp, the comrade fled. I did not receive any further news about him. Because of the stupidity and naivety of a woman at such a time, Nyome got into the prison camp and suffered the fate of all captured Red Army soldiers, 99 percent of whom were shot or starved to death. So this is how Nyome's life ended in July 1941.

There was not a bit of food at home. After we left our parents and sister alone, they could not stock up. I had to look for work as soon as I had finished that long walk. I get a job with a German, whose room I have to fit out, and I steal half of the flour,

---

(1)   As for "Stein's Factory" watch this film
https://www.youtube.com/watch?v=5Gk6ClhJOTY

Page 29

he gives me for clay[making] and take it home. It will be a feast of joy, we already have something to eat! A few "cookies" instead of bread, and flour boiled in water, this is the food in those days.

Every day you have to get out of the house, squeeze in between thousands who want to get work just for a meal. Three of us go outside, me, father and Beybe. Sometimes one of us gets a job, sometimes none. The one who makes it eats up and brings the leftovers home for the others.

The Yellow Patch—the Greatest Shame of the Twentieth Century

Next to the Judenrat there is already a new notice: "All Jews from the age of 14 up to the highest age, men and women, must wear a yellow Star of David 10 centimeters wide and long on their hearts and on their shoulders. Jews without a yellow Star of David will be shot!" This again hits everyone like a bomb. One of the Judenrat goes out into the streets and shows how the yellow patch must be worn. Everyone looks for yellow linen, one dyes white linen yellow, but is ashamed to go out on the streets. Therefore, many just sit at home for weeks. But it all helps nothing, if you want to go out, you have to turn on [the patch], otherwise you can pay with your life. The Jews themselves have to make sure that everyone wears it. One from each house puts it on, goes out into the street, and comes back shortly after. I can't go out with it. It's terrible to see everyone walking with the patches on their shoulders, and in the front additionally sticks the other half of the pain. You try to make it beautiful, but nothing comes of it - a patch remains a patch. Gradually you get used to it, too, because there is already a bigger worry: Jews are being locked up in a ghetto! We absolutely do not know how we will live there, what we can eat, because already people are starving.

Page 30

The Ghetto

The whole Jewish population is now occupied by one issue: Where will the ghetto be? How will people live there? How many streets? What will one work with? What will one live on? But "the German" doesn't leave much time for reflection. Unpleasant decrees are pouring in, one after the other. One is just still in the process of clarifying how one will live with the one decree, when the next one already comes. In the four years of German rule, there will not be a minute's peace!

Jews carry beds and bundles of belongings from all corners of the city. All move to Kupiecka, Nowy Świat, Tsheple [Ciepła] Street and the whole surrounding area, which is not the ugliest of Bialystok. It is said that it was the Judenrat that enforced it should be in a nice area of the city. It cost money again to bribe the city commander. The Jews themselves build a large fence in all the streets of two and a half meters high, and half a meter of barbed wire is added on top. Two gates are built as an exit, one on Kupiecka and one on Yurovetske [Jurowiecka] Street. A small square on Zhabe [Żabia, Frog] Street serves as a cemetery, which, if you look, is getting more crowded with every passing day. When someone dies a "normal" death-that is, dies because of the conditions in the ghetto— they say, "that Jew is a wise man!"

All Poles and non-Jews must leave the streets designated for the ghetto. They are given apartments in another part of the city. The 60,000 Jews are herded across to their neighborhood. They are not allowed to occupy more than 3 meters per person, but gladly less. Two or three families move into a single room. They are separated by a door or thick walls. All Bote-Medroshim [Houses of Studies], all stores, where there is space, are occupied. There is no place for the population. School buildings, which are located in the ghetto, are also occupied—there is no need to study anymore... Furniture is carried to the attics—there is no place for it in the room—

Page 31

or is left in the former apartment. The richer Jews rent carriages, for which the Poles take a piano or things from the beautiful bedroom. "It doesn't matter," they say, "you don't need it anymore." The burned-out Jews carry nothing with them; the poorer population from Khanaykes [Chanajki] or Pyaskes [Piaski], carry as much as they can on their shoulders or on a handcart.

In the "ghetto"—a horrible picture. Everybody is dragging. Small children, old Jews and Jewish women, who were bedridden before and can hardly walk, have to carry bedding, beds, dishes and wood. That' s how it goes for a few days. At the same time, Germans with cameras have positioned themselves in the streets and are taking pictures. All the courtyards are full of dumped furniture and things. There are fights, unwanted people come in and you have to live with them, Poles join in, beat and rob in the yards, and no one can defend themselves. But, everything is transported across. The towage comes to a halt, the fence is put up, we are already sitting there locked in, with a guard of Germans around us, and can no longer go out.

Before the time of the move, Poles come and bring a little potatoes, greens and ask for suits of clothes each for 20 kilos of potatoes. I myself sell a suit of clothes and shoes and get 25 kilos of potatoes, 3 kilos of peas and a little flour. Most of the time you stock up for a few weeks. What you have, you give away to get a little bit of food. We don't know how long we have to stock up for.

You are not allowed to go further than the fence. After 9 o'clock in the evening, you are not allowed to go out on the street at all. At night, people meet and talk about how they will live under such conditions. There are thefts, mostly of food. Everyone lives close together, one blames it on the other, one does not know each other and so it comes to arguments, until people no longer speak to each other in their apartments.

A Jewish police force is to be established. Anyone who wants to can register for it. It is rumored which elements want to become policemen now, probably

Page 32

the worst, from the underworld. But, when the Jewish police, who call themselves by the German name "Ordnungsdienst", show up with their green hats, everyone is surprised: it is precisely the scholars, the graduates of high schools and merchants who are known as "intelligentsia".

Fighting for a Bite of Bread

Some of the people go to work outside the ghetto early in the morning, with slips of paper in their hands that allow them to pass through the gate. On the way back they bring some vegetables they bought or got at work. Inside, behind the gate, the family of the lucky person stands waiting to see what he will bring from work today. A new kind of poor emerges: Those who ask something from the one who brings something inside. Early in the morning the Germans come and take Jews to work. At least girls go, men are afraid. Maybe one will not come back. The girls try to please.

"Today I put on the blouse, the German took me and not the other one"... "I am blond, he always chooses me"...These are the conversations you hear at that time.

In the ghetto, a pood [16,38 kg] of flour costs $3. Bread is baked sequentially in the bakeries that are located in the ghetto. The person who bakes takes a loaf of bread for himself from the baked goods. Gradually, more and more Jews go out to work. Factories are established in the ghetto where work is done for the Germans. Everyone has to work, there is forced labor for children from 14 years old and older men and women up to 70 years old. Everyone wants to get a job outside the ghetto, because there you meet with the population, which trades for leather and suits for food, which you carry in [to the ghetto]. One sells more to another, and gradually a trade begins between the people, which causes the price of food to fall.

A Jew who goes to work is given 250 grams of bread for 2 days by the Judenrat.

Page 33

People with handcarts drive flour from the Judenrat to the bakeries and also earn something. Others risk their lives. Children as young as 10 sneak out through the fence onto the street and run into a village to exchange something for food. Leaving the ghetto is sentenced to death. That's why children go, because it's easier for them to sneak out. The one who doesn't work in the ghetto sells his stuff to the one who works outside, and so they both earn. One gets edibles for his stuff and the other gets something for carrying the edibles in and doing the transaction. In this way, one gradually gets used to it, and soon even a small store opens. Here people bring in surplus goods, and the store then sells everything individually to the population. On the "Nayvelt" [Nowy Świat], Prage's garden, a market is created where middlemen buy in large quantities what they then resell at high individual prices. However, as gradually more and more go out to work and bring more in, products become cheaper. Life, you can say, normalizes, provided that there are no more unpleasant dispositions.

At the Entrance and Exit of the Ghetto

Early in the morning at 6 o'clock, those who work outside the ghetto begin to go out. They have a piece of paper in their hands on which is written on which street they work. At the gate there are two Germans with rifles and two unarmed Jewish policemen, checking and feeling everyone to make sure they are not carrying anything out to sell. People used to put on good suits under their dirty work clothes or tie on pieces of leather or tablecloths to sell them at work. For many, the things are found, they are taken away from them and they are beaten for it, others manage to smuggle [things] through. One asks the other, "[is today] a good watch? Can something be brought out?" If yes, one goes off with it, if no, one carries nothing through that day. It happens that on one day one of the guards does not make a search, but the other one does very well,

Page 34

then everyone crowds to the "good German", getting punches for shoving.

After going through hell, you have to walk on the road where the corresponding markers are. In case you are caught on another road, you will be beaten and searched. If something is found on a person, he is arrested. For a whole day, Jews, children and women, drag themselves along the pavement with bundles, which they carry into the ghetto at lunchtime, from 12 to 2 pm. When you meet a Gestapo agent, you are stopped and everything is taken from you, even money. When you go to work, you are not allowed to take any money with you, because "what does a Jew need money for, when he is forbidden to buy anything, and where does he get the money from, when he is not paid at work"? Patrols of Germans and Poles move along the street. When they see you with a yellow patch on the asphalt of the street, they call you over and ask, "what are you doing here when you work on a different street?" If they only take your money and the bundle you carry, they are good Germans, because others take you to the Gestapo, where you get 20 lashes on your bare bottom. After that you cannot sit for months, but that does not stop anyone; under such conditions you have to continue to make purchases.

No sooner have you bought a bit to eat than you have to bribe your German employer with a few marks so that he doesn't take it away and let you carry it home after work. Fats are carried on your body, under your clothes, but the Germans at the gate pat you down from head to toe and administer blows if you don't stop immediately. Next to the gate are sacks of potatoes, kilos of butter, bottles of cooking oil, chickens. Others carry their goods back and hide them in ruins for the next day. Perhaps there will be a better guard tomorrow, although that is rarely the case. The Germans take away whole carloads of food and sell that somewhere. But if someone managed to smuggle something through, one of the Jewish police comes and demands a part of it, after all, he also has to live. If you don't give him anything, he sends you back to the guard and everything is taken away. This is their income...

Page 35

The higher [Jewish] police, the so-called commanders, who are not at the gate, arrest you and make a bigger deal out of it. A group of five people was formed from Zelikovitsh, Kvater, Fin and two others, who usually arrest people in the basement of the Judenrat building. There was the prison that they called "Sing-Sing". It was where they used to slaughter poultry, on Yatke [Butcher Shop] Street. [The group] would usually come at night, claiming that the Gestapo was calling for you. From there, we knew, one never came back. One of the five used to claim that if you gave him a hundred dollars, he would bribe the Germans and they wouldn't need to lead you to the Gestapo. They often arrested communists and demanded a lot of money. If the Gestapo actually demanded an arrest, then it was all for nothing. The point was that they acted on their own initiative to extort money. A person who bought his freedom from them had to hide all the time, because in their impudence they would otherwise arrest him two or three times.

As for Zelikovitsh, however, these were still minor offenses. As an intermediary between the ghetto and the Gestapo, Zelikovitsh helped himself to a lot of the things that the Judenrat had to deliver to the Germans. He took home skins and silk fabric, but at the same time demanded on his own initiative whatever he wanted. He reached such a status in those days that the Germans chose him as the best Jew and allowed him to go without the yellow patch. However, his business affairs grew larger and larger until they burst. He fell out of favor with Shimanski, who was the city president at the time, and on the occasion of his visit he gave him a beating and painted a yellow patch on his front and back. He conducted an audit [of Zelikovitsh] and found in his apartment, hidden in the walls, a lot of gold, silk and cloth goods. He was arrested and died in prison. The other four comrades were sent to a concentration camp.

Page 36

However, they managed to free themselves with the help of money.

Such people—the scum of their own people, who, in view of the already hard, simply inhuman conditions in the ghetto, made life even more difficult for others, were not few in number. The lower-ranking [Jewish] police also used to arrest people, claiming that they were not working and would therefore be put to hard labor. Every day this happened. Now, since the wealthier ones usually bought their way out, they arrested those who did have work. One could not even go out on the street on Sunday for fear of being arrested at work. Most of the time it cost money to get free. This was the income of the Jewish police.

The Judenrat

The Judenrat was composed essentially of the former functionaries of the Jewish community who remained after all the arsons and arrests of the Germans: The Rabbi, Dr. Roz[en]man, Engineer Barash, Subotnik, Goldberg, Vishnyevski [Wisniewski] and others. Barash was to be glorified as a man who became the savior of the Bialystok Jews from greatest extermination. But after he delivered people to be shot, he became very compromised and lost a lot of his authority.

The work of the Judenrat consisted of giving in to the Germans in everything they demanded; even in "selling" a part of the Jews for the price that another part of the Jews remained alive. And they [actually] believed that this would succeed. They wanted to gain time at all costs until the liberation of the ghetto by the Red Army. They did not believe the German who said, "in case we lose at 12 o'clock, we will murder all but one Jew 5 minutes to 12!" The Judenrat established factories in the ghetto, implemented

Page 37

all the new machines and created huge tailor shops to sew uniforms for the German Wehrmacht, plus shoemaker shops that sewed boots. There were also belt factories and laundries that washed German linen from the front. The greatest tragedy for the workers was when later Jewish clothes from Treblinka arrived for washing, in which the documents could still be seen. The ghetto was turned into a factory where one had to work for 250 grams of bread for two days. However, one did not even get this, if one did not meet the estimated standard. If you were too slow at work, your ration was taken away and it was said, as we were told, "death to him who does not work!" Even older women, old men and 14-year-old children sat with knitting needles and made gloves and socks for them for the winter. Work was done in three rotations, and those who just didn't have a place in the factory had to work at home. So our little sister Raytsele, at the age of 14, had to knit gloves for the Germans, a whole ten hours a day. The standard was calculated in such a way that you could not fulfill it with less time. Afterwards you had to take [the product] to the factory and show the department manager that you had made it well. If it was bad, you had to improve it in your "free time" and did not get a portion of bread. German private individuals also set up factories in the ghetto, they took advantage of the free Jewish labor hands. Giving a little porridge for work was enough, and they were already considered the best workplaces.

In general, it was mainly the richer people who worked in the ghetto, because one could not live on what one got for the work. The poorer part had to work outside the ghetto, doing superhumanly heavy jobs, plus receiving beatings. The one positive aspect was that you could usually buy something and smuggle it into the ghetto, thereby earning a bit. However, since on the

Page 38

way the goods were usually confiscated, the fence was undermined in certain places, which were only little guarded. It was agreed with the children that they would wait there and smuggle the things over. Large quantities of food were also brought in on carts of dung or in cesspools. After the dirt had been poured out and the containers washed out, meat, flour and other things were put in. Of course, the Jewish policeman and the German at the gate had to be bribed to let the carts through. The arrival of winter brought a new problem: wood was needed to cook something. However, they did not let anyone bring in wood and even from the factories it was not allowed to take the smallest board. The Jewish police usually searched each worker as he left the factory, even looking in the pockets of his clothes, and threw out of the factory anyone they found with only a few [larger] shavings.

Only sawdust and wood shavings were allowed. So life dragged on until the first winter of 1941, when a new unpleasant order ["gzeyre"] turned up.

The New Gzeyre "Pruzhene" [Pruzhany]

Pruzhany is a shtetl next to the Bialovyezher [Białowieża] forests, far from Bialystok. The German Gestapo leader Fridel ordered that twelve thousand Jews be sent there. After visits from all the commissions and mediators who had looked around the ghetto, the Gestapo said, "there are too many Jews in the ghetto!"

Very often Germans used to come to the Judenrat in taxis. On this occasion, the Jewish police ordered everyone to stay at home and not to be seen. Barash then usually drove out in a hackney cab and showed [the Germans] how diligently the Jews were working in the factories. When they [the Germans] came in, they would be given presents and measurements were taken for boots and clothing. But this did not help. Their answer was short: "Too many Jews in the ghetto, the non-productive ones must be deported!"

Page 39

The Judenrat sets to work: a special office is created to register all skilled workers. The street next to the Judenrat is black with people; all become "skilled workers". Suddenly, a second rumor, exchanged under the seal of secrecy, but everyone knows about it immediately: those who work outside the ghetto will not be sent out. Immediately, everyone is hunting for a job outside the ghetto. Sinister elements take advantage of this: They demand money for such a certificate. It becomes clear to everyone that the Jewish police will not be deported. Overnight, fresh policemen grow out of the ground, like mushrooms ["bitkes"] after the rain. They already had a name, "the 50 Dolerdikn [Dollar's]", because only for 50 dollars and powerful patronage you got a green police hat.

The days go by and the rumors change. A rumor is going by that you can save elderly people who are unable to work, if you attribute them to a person who is working [outside]. People are rushing around headless, my aunt Shifre comes running, asking me to register her [together with my name]. I try to make her understand that this registration will not help unless you get protection or have money to "pay" the people in charge. You can have the best job, and yet you are sent out. But at such a time you cannot convince people, when you are in danger of drowning, you hold on to the straw. I take her to Judenrat, stand in line for a whole day, and then have her register on my work slip.

[The day of] deportation is approaching. Every evening policemen carry out notes from the Judenrat that one should line up at dawn on Fabritshne [Fabryczna] Street, where a special gate has been erected.The notes are distributed according to the alphabet and everyone is now in expectation; also to my letter, "K" -Kot, a note arrives. I come back from work outside the ghetto as usual, but I don't bring more, we will at least be able to eat what is left. My heart is pounding as I enter the ghetto through the gate, I am already tired of answering everyone who envies me my work and asks me if I already have someone registered on my paper.

Page 40

Coming home, everyone is sitting there dejectedly, their things thrown about like after a pogrom. Everything is clear to me and I don't even ask. I don't ask for food either. The paper from the Judenrat is on the table; the family has to line up at 5 o'clock the next morning. Even Nyome, who was no longer in the ghetto, was not forgotten by the Judenrat (apparently, he had received money from someone for having Nyome entered in his place). Neighbors and acquaintances come in, don't even say good evening, stand in a corner with a sad face and try to comfort: You are working, what does the Judenrat want from you?

I run away to my workplace to ask the Germans to sign that they need me. But I don't meet anyone. Father meets the German [employer] at his workplace, and the latter gives him

My parents

a certificate. I run to the Judenrat, shouting that I work and am a professional, but there are so many people there, all shouting, each with good arguments. All the rooms are full, the Jewish police won't let anyone in, there is pushing. But it all doesn't help. The answer is: it will be decided on the spot; you have to join the line.

I come back home; we receive advice not to go to line up.

Page 41

But, how to do that, when the family's existence in the ghetto is already canceled, the police seize them, detain them and put them up for transport anyway. We pack as much as we can. We have to leave many things behind; at that moment, there is not even someone to whom we can sell them.

There is heavy frost on the road and fine snowflakes are falling. For the last time we heat the room well, we have to leave the wood anyway. Father sits silently next to the stove and warms himself. He coughs a lot, as usual. Raytsele, nestled on the empty bed against our mother, looks at me, looking for a rescue. Mother reminds me, "Did you pack Nyome's suit, too?" It is the only thing she has left of Nyome. In the hardest days of hunger she did not let me sell it but said, "when he comes back, he should at least have something to wear..."

The clock gongs louder than usual after every hour, for it is quiet in the parlor. We only exchange glances. Now the walls are talking, we have been together so long, so long, and now...

The clock strikes 5. It is still dark on the street. We all get up, the neighbors we say goodbye to, shed a tear; they console us with the fact that nobody knows who will have to go next. Those who bring us there take the bundles from us and we, agitated and bitter, leave our home. The furniture and many things remain behind. The pictures on the walls will bear witness that people lived here.

On the streets only people with luggage walk, you don't recognize anyone, everyone is excited, groaning, only their footsteps creak in the snow. We reach Fabrithsne [Fabryczna] Street. There are people from the police who let through only those whom they have called. The others they drive away with sticks. A policeman takes the paper from us and directs us to the place where we have to wait. We put our luggage on the ground. All along Fabryczna Street there are snowed-in people, knocking one foot against the other; there are old people with gray beards, sick people and also babies. We hear

Page 42

Jewish women groaning, old Jews reciting psalms and soothing words of endearment from mothers to their young children. All of this is intermixed with beating and shouting from the Germans.

The gate opens and trucks drive in. We are told that the Judenrat had negotiated that we be transported by cars and not have to run on foot (a great boon paid for with much money and favors!). The Germans, along with a Judenrat foreman, start checking the lists. People beg the Germans, they show papers and signatures where they work and that they are needed at work. But, only at a hint from the person from the Judenrat, the Germans let go of someone. The rest are pushed on a truck. The Germans, meanwhile, deal out blows; never do they refrain!...Someone comes up to me. I, father and Beybe are standing, below us, on top of the luggage, are sitting Mom and Reitsele. Father shows his paper and begs, I show my paper and say nothing. How could I beg a bandit?

Mom starts to cry and Raytsele, looking at her, also cries. Seeing the scene and the chaos all around, here letting people go home and there pushing them into cars, I grab the packed things and say to Beybe, "Don't wait for the German's decision, grab packs and run from the square!" Across the street lived my comrade. I threw all the things in to him and hurried home with the family through back alleys and courtyards. Everyone rejoices; we are back in our four walls; father at the stove, the others on the empty beds, which are so dear to us now…

All the other Jews, except for small exceptions, are hoisted onto the trucks and drive towards Pruzhany, leaving behind a lot of bundles. (Shifre with the aunt [sic!] were also taken away). Before Pruzhany they have to go through a checkpoint. The trucks stop in front of a small house. The Jews are ordered to get out and go into the house one by one. There the Germans order them to strip stark naked and take away

Page 43

what they like. The naked people are beaten, including the women, and they are brought to Pruzhany, traumatized and deprived.

In the shtetl they meet very few Jews. The entire peasant population was taken away by the Germans so that the partisans in the Białowieża forest would not encounter anyone from whom they could obtain food. The Jews occupy these homes but have neither employment nor anything to support themselves. They try to return through various routes. Many of them are seized and arrested. Those who make it back to the Bialystok ghetto arrive with frostbitten feet and other limbs. They do not even find a place to live, because their old apartments are already occupied. They have to avoid saying they are from Pruzhany, so they exchange their surnames and say they are from other places.

The deportations to Pruzhany last for three weeks, and a total of over 8000 people are taken away. Towards the end, a great demoralization arises, because one realizes that the Judenrat selects only poor people and workers from the population, who have no bribe money and no protection. So people stop lining up until one fine early morning the transports are stopped. It is claimed this was achieved by the Judenrat through bribery. In reality, however, this is the result of demoralization, and because, moreover, a sufficient number had already been transported away.

After the evacuations, the ghetto is reduced in size, several streets are excluded (half of Polne [Polna] and part of Zhidovske [Židovska] Street), the Jews, God forbid, should not live too spacious. The opinion spread by the Judenrat is solidifying again that one must work; if we worked more, it would save us from a new "gzeyre".

Page 44

The First Activity of the Underground Organization

However, a small part of the people in the ghetto, mostly the youth, have been brought up in a revolutionary spirit and make a different statement: *"We can be saved if we resist, if we go to the forest to fight, unite with all the others who are fighting against the Germans, this is a hard way but an honorable, more safe and humane way that puts us on a par with all the fighting peoples."*

This was understood only by the communist youth and parts of the Hashomer Hatzair. In the most critical moment of our people they united to fight against the enemy; not with work, which only helped people to beg for their lives, but with weapons in their hands to defend their lives!

There also came people of other [political] directions, not as a whole organization, but privately, with the recommendation of acquaintances who guaranteed us that this person is not a traitor. In case of betrayal, the rule was that one would be shot by one's own comrades. In the beginning, the comrades who joined the organization had very poor military training and hardly any had served in the military. This is the greatest tragedy of the Jewish people. People always looked at military service and its training as a kind of "gzeyre", and those who could avoid military service did so. Now we were feeling the effects. However, we comrades had a sound mind and the conviction that there was no other way for us.

Where were we going to get weapons? How was that to be organized? These were the most difficult questions for us. Around Bialystok the forests were small, we heard nothing of partisans and

Page 45

could not make any contact with them. Our organization decides to form a partisan group ourselves and to test sending out the first comrades. While we are mobilizing the people, our number increases and we divide the ghetto into districts, in each of which a group is formed, from which only one leader meets with the leader of another group. We set up a radio receiver and report on political news at small meetings. But still the Germans are getting ahead. There is no glimmer of hope.

Given our fear of the Judenrat, which arrests those like us for allegedly "bringing harm to the Jews in the ghetto," we work in the utmost secrecy. Even Beybe (my brother), who also belonged to our organization, initially told me nothing about it. Only before I go out to a partisan group does he tell me that he already knows that I will have to go out shortly. Every member was given the duty to steal necessary parts for rifles from his workplace.

And so I steal various parts of rifles from where I work, hide them and carry them to the ghetto bit by bit. Depending on the possibility, all the comrades do it (if one is caught, of course, he gets the death penalty). In the ghetto the parts are assembled. Those who work in the locksmith's shop in the ghetto, under the leadership of our comrade Farber, secretly produce grenades and smuggle them from the factory to our organization. In this way everything is prepared. My comrade, Motl Tsheremashne, works for the Gestapo; he makes a key to the entrance door to the weapons room, steals out two rifles and pushes them through the fence to his wife, with whom he had arranged this beforehand. Each member risks 100% of his life in the smallest thing he does. So on such conditions, only a small part of the youth, the revolutionary youth, is working. Girls also help. Girls,

Page 46

who work for Germans, steal bandages and medicines. Everything is prepared under the greatest risks, we have to beware of the Judenrat, the Jewish police and Jewish spies, who are not missing either.

For many Jews our point of view is still strange. They were quicker to follow the Judenrat's idea that time could be gained by working, although it is clear to see how "living pieces" were torn out of the ghetto and how thousands of the Jews of Bialystok were already missing; of whom it is not even known how they perished. The Judenrat tells everyone that it means nothing, that it will pass. They, the members of the Judenrat, are robbing the Jews of the ghetto, making a good day of it with the loot, and they don't feel comfortable fighting. They think that they can save their own lives by the death of others. But the organization educates its comrades and manages to gradually break down the propaganda of the Judenrat.

There are exterminations and shootings in Slonim, Baranovitsh [Baranovichi], and Volkovisk. Jews come running from mass graves, where they buried whole shtetls alive (the Germans even economized their bullets for the Jews). We believe the people who arrive and report, but the Judenrat keeps feeding the ghetto the same fairy tales, that these are lies and "we stay alive, we just have to work, work some more. No harm is done to those who work".

On the occasion of the "few" murders of thousands of Jews that happen in Bialystok, the organization cannot yet act; it is simply still very young and does not yet have a "foot in the door" with leaders who can obtain information. However, when our comrade Joschke is arrested, we help him escape from the concentration camp, and after he tells us everything that happened, we decide to resist when there is a shooting in the Bialystok ghetto. All preparations for this are already underway.

The help from the "Polish street" is minimal, almost non-existent. The Polish socialists are silent, doing nothing; the nationalists are

Page 47

against the Jews, helping the Germans. We get support only from the Russians who stayed in place after failing to get into the Soviet Union, and from the P.P.R. (Polska Partia Robotnitsha), the Polish Communist Party. But their number is very small and everyone had to be extremely careful, because just for a meeting of a Jew with a Pole, they used to shoot the Jew and his whole family that they found with him.

New Year in Ghetto

In the ghetto, not a week goes by without certain arrests to "keep it quiet". However, until the great extermination, when one has already stepped on one's parents, brothers and sisters with one's own feet, and one has picked them up from the streets with one's own hands and placed them in mass graves, until this time, to express it in the ghetto language, everything runs "normally" and "nothing at all" happens. Not even when the Gestapo leader Friedel demands that three Jews be hanged.

Early in the morning we all go to work with the only concern of being able to buy something and bring it in on the way back from work, but, when we return today, each of us cringes: no one is standing by the gate, no one has to wait, the Germans do not search, there is no line in front of the gate. What's going on? Another news, fitting for New Year, New Year's Eve? It must have been quiet for too long!

As we walk in, we don't see a single soul on the street, a consternation grips us, it chokes us. "What has happened," I ask a Jew I finally meet as I sadly walk on. "Today three Jews will be hanged in the ghetto," is his answer. Continuing, I see: Yes, it is the truth, a gallows is already being erected opposite the Judenrat, on Kupiecka Street. It is quiet on the streets. You only hear the banging of the hammers building the gallows. What a good beginning of the new year 1942!

Page 48

Why are the Jews being hanged, and who will be hanged, I ask myself, and later learn the answer. There were many workplaces where you were severely beaten up on the day you were assigned to work there. Moreover, at these workplaces you could not buy anything to take to the ghetto for a piece of bread. One could not last long at these workplaces. But Jews had to come to these workplaces as well, and the Judenrat had to provide the necessary number of workers every day.

So the Labor Office used to determine that the people who worked in a factory in the ghetto would go to such a [bad] job one day a week, because the work in the ghetto was considered easier work. People worked there without control by the Germans; there were only Jewish supervisors. The richer Jews, however, did not want to work for Germans outside the ghetto one day a week. They were allowed to "hire" a person in their name (such a person was called "Malekh", [angel]). Such a "Malekh" used to cost 5 or 10 marks per working day, calculated according to the number of blows that awaited him at work. For 5 marks one usually got a loaf of bread in the ghetto. However, this was very little for a person with a family. Therefore, it was common to "take" (swipe) something at work if possible. The three people also worked as "Angels" at such a workplace, an edible oil factory that was formerly in Jewish and now in German hands. A few days before the New Year, a balance was taken and it was found that money was missing. The German director was to be arrested. However, the latter knew that the workers usually put nut kernels in their jacket pockets when they left the factory, but this had no relevance to the deficit. This, however, gave him an idea of how to wriggle out of the matter, namely by blaming the deficit on the Jews. He called the Gestapo and instructed them to search the Jews before they left the factory, and sure enough, they found a few nut kernels in everyone's pockets. They were

Page 49

immediately arrested, taken to the ghetto and accused of being responsible for the deficit in the factory.

Three young fellows were sentenced to be hanged directly on New Year's Eve, directly opposite the Judenrat, a present on New Year's Day 1942. The Jewish police had to carry out the hanging. The other seven Jews who had worked in the same factory had to stand by and watch. They did not know that they would not be hanged but waited for it as well.

The young innocent victims were hung for three hours. No one left his house, the streets were empty, everyone sat and talked about the incident. The families of the prisoners stifle the pain inside, you cannot cry out, and to whom? The very next day, the first day of the new year, the ghetto is already gripped by a new grief: An innocent young woman, not long after her wedding, has been killed by a German who shot through her window.

One thing follows another, there is no time to stick to one event when the next one is already happening, especially with an even greater number of victims.

The "Gzeyre" Volkovisk

Gestapo leader Friedel does not pause the slightest time. After New Year's Day he demands to hand over 300 women for hard labor in the concentration camp of Volkovisk. This is the first time that women are specifically demanded for hard labor. In the past, people used to say that "women are lucky" because wherever there were seizures and shootings, only men were involved. Girls used to work for Germans and support the families. They were more likely to be let through at the gate and not searched; but now there were no more "unproductive persons" to deport;

Page 50

the Germans no longer had such an excuse as justification, so now they turned to women.

As is the way of the Judenrat, it sees to it that the order is obeyed. He decides that from each factory ten percent of the girls and women who have no children should be delivered.

They are drawn by lot, but needless to say, only among those who have no money to give to the people who do business with Jewish blood in the saddest days of the ghetto.

Of course, the people concerned do not enter voluntarily, because who wants to go to a concentration camp without knowing whether they will

Raytsele

come back? All the girls and women go into hiding, sleeping at night not in their rooms but in cellars built especially for them. The Jewish police cordoned off entire streets and made house searches. They take the girls out from under the beds and from the attics and bring them to the Judenrat prison. Brawls break out between women and the Jewish police. On Kupiecka Street they surround the factories and drag the girls away from work. The girls jump through the windows and back doors; the tumult continues for three weeks. Some

Page 51

women are bought out of prison. This causes great fuss among everyone. Mothers demonstrate in front of the Judenrat demanding that their daughters be freed, but without result.

Our family is also affected again. Raytsele, my little 14-year-old sister, who is just taking her first steps into the world and could have enjoyed her life in normal times, can only develop with difficulty, and now she additionally has to hide at night in the cellar I made for her. At every movement of the door or [audible] search for girls, she turns pale and looks at me with her black eyes that say, "I am young, and I want to live, dear Srolke, save me!" I then keep silent—what to say to her? —and avoid looking at her, but her young eyes, full of life, speak to me, demanding without words. Such a feeling stays in your mind and torments you when you remember; constantly you see those eyes before you.... There, maybe it is easier to see dead people, even if they are close to you, than to be such a helpless "protector" of someone who looks at you, and keep silent! I cannot describe these agonizing feelings.

The day of the deportation of the imprisoned women has arrived. Carriages are brought, the police lead the girls out of the prison and load them onto the carriages. With their hair disheveled and dirty because they had not been able to wash for days, frightened and struggling with their fate, the girls still reassure their mothers, who run after the carts with their hands out, screaming and crying. Painful scenes occur. Some girls jump down from the carts and run away, but the police chase after them, catch them and forcefully push them back onto the cart. One girl lies on the ground, wrestling with death. The mother throws herself in convulsions at the murderers; everyone feels the women's pain.

The mothers could still accompany their children to the gate of the ghetto, but not further. Two Germans with guns in their hands opened the gate and let the carriages out. In the ghetto, everything remains

Page 52

as it has been. Everyone remains in their grief (Raytsele managed to hide and she stayed at home).

A few months pass, and the mothers demand that those who were deported to work be exchanged, as the Judenrat had promised at the time. The mothers demonstrate, protest; the police disperse them and beat the demonstrators to the bone. Further arrests cause the earlier demands to be forgotten; one must continue to hide.

Osovyets (Osowiec)

When night falls and you have to go to sleep because it's closing time, the night life of the ghetto begins. As soon as everything is quiet, people sneak out of their houses, start breaking fences to bring the wood into the kitchen, even destroy [wooden] stairs at night if one is not careful... Still later at night the police go over the houses, drag people out of bed and send them to the Gestapo: they need hundreds of people for the concentration camp in Osowiec.

Well, they don't grab me. From the workplace they don't send me to a camp, but to a German to paint his apartment. To go there by train, I need a special permit with 20 signatures, which takes a whole day. A German leads me everywhere. I walk on the cobblestones, he walks on the sidewalk. Even on the train, a German accompanies me; I am not allowed to ride alone. Everyone looks at me—I don't know whether they feel sorry for me or are disgusted by me—it's one of those things: a Jew with a patch is riding on the train!

Arriving in Osowiec together with another comrade, we do not live in a camp but work in the apartment of a German. The camp where the Bialystok Jews were working in the most difficult conditions was not far from me. The Jews had to endure a lot,

Page 53

including on the part of the Poles who were sent to the same camp.

I was free after work, and my only interest was to go there to listen to the Russian prisoners sing. In the evening they sang Russian songs full of sadness, as well as with hope. I used to listen to the songs until late at night. It was a little easier to bear here than in the ghetto, because there was no fence and even the patches had been taken from me. However, after two weeks, I was taken back to Bialystok, while the other Jews who stayed behind in the concentration camp never returned again.

For Work to Germany

In the ghetto, no profession is considered safe anymore. In the past, skilled workers were envied because nothing was done to them. Now, however, skilled workers are being dragged out of their beds and deported to Germany. The police have learned: What is the point of blocking off the streets during the day and struggling to grab people, when you can get lists of skilled workers, bricklayers, printers and others at the registration office, who can be dragged out of their beds at night without causing a commotion?

No place is left to rest, neither by day nor by night. One is never safe from sorrow and suffering, one lives constantly with fear, at every creak of a door or the running of a person. It is enough to see a person running away or someone knocking on the door at night. Then the youngsters run to hide in the cellar or under the beds and let the old mother open the door. Later, however, the parents are arrested when their children are not found.

Thus begins the winter of 1942-1943.

Page 54

The Extermination in the Province around Bialystok
(The Destruction of Bialystok)

In the ghetto the air is indescribably oppressive. From Bielsk come trucks with remaining Jews, obviously professionals. The rest were taken to Treblinka, and some of them were shot on the spot. The "lucky" ones who are brought here are the only ones left from their families. They tell about the whole fate of the events. From everywhere, also from Grodno, Jews are brought here with the same ingenious methods and with the help of Jews. Here obviously must be "the lucky ghetto" where they are allowed to stay.

However, on a certain morning, when "life" awakens in the ghetto with the walk to work outside the gate and the new poor in the ghetto, women and children, stand on the street corners, breathe into their frozen hands and shamefully ask for alms, the ghetto is stirred up by a new event:

The ghetto is surrounded by the Gestapo; every ten meters there are armed Germans with machine guns and grenades in their hands. We are not let out to work. Gripped by terror, one asks the other, *"S-s-so n-n-now with us, t-t-too?"*

It's hard to describe what a person thinks and how they feel at a moment like that. One runs to find out what is going on.

Finally, we learn that all the Jews from the surrounding towns are being taken away, Bialystokers themselves are not touched. We breathe out more freely, although we have little confidence.

The Germans have confiscated all the farmers' horse-drawn wagons to drive into the small towns at night. All Jews are herded out of their homes onto the wagons, leaving all their belongings in the houses. They are taken to assembly points at train stations. Many are also driven forward on foot. Those who do not

Page 55

come along quickly enough are shot. During the week when the deportation of Jews from the small towns continues, the whole road around Bialystok is covered with corpses of old women and men.

A large part of those rounded up have been taken to the former "10th Lithuanian Uhlan Regiment" [10 Pułk Ułanów Litewskich] and thrown into the horse stables there, which were without windows and doors. Small babies, women and men were exposed to the frost there for weeks until those who had not perished from cold and hunger and were able to save themselves from being shot, were loaded into wagons and deported to Treblinka. Only a few are ransomed by the Judenrat, which states that they are Bialystokers. When Barash comes with a truck and calls out certain family names, hundreds run to him; no wonder, they all want to save themselves.

A certain part of the Jews from the small towns managed to escape when they were led into the forest. However, the conditions in the forests around Bialystok at that time were very difficult for people without weapons, and moreover in winter, when there is snow and you cannot walk because footprints can be seen. Partisans used to prepare food during the summer, but the Jews, who could only save their bare lives, had to go straight to the peasants and, of course, pay strange prices. Moreover, they were sometimes robbed by the Polish partisans, who used to take off their boots and often even shot them. Many Jews perished because of these hard conditions and unpreparedness. There were hardly any Russian partisans in our area, only small groups of Russians with few weapons, fugitives from captivity, but even they used to move eastward to avoid the Polish partisans, who robbed and fought Jews and Russians.

Of the large groups of Jews, only individuals remained in the partisan groups and endured until the end. The fact that the

Page 56

Bialystok ghetto remained in place hindered the perseverance of people who would have been better off deciding to stay in the forest. After months of wandering in the woods and streets, many tried to enter the Bialystok ghetto, but they had to pass through the guarded perimeter and were shot if they tried to cross the fence, or they were captured and thrown into prison, from where they were taken by trucks south of the city [Bialystok] to Novisholk [Nowosiółki] and shot or buried alive.

In this way more than half a million Jews perished and the province was "judenrein" [cleansed of Jews] by the end of 1942.

––––––––––

Before the time of liquidation, the ghetto was surrounded by Germans. The small stores had to close and food had become unaffordable. But, no one worried about food, everyone was only concerned with how to hide in order to stay alive. Every night you could hear the banging of hammers, and every morning when you came to the yards, you saw fresh piles of sand. They had been created after digging hiding places and shoveling out the sand. We had pooled the money with our neighbors and spent the last Mark to build a hiding place. Another cellar was dug out from the neighbor's cellar. A new city was built in the cellars, in the attics and in the double walls. During this period, Bialystok still escaped with a scare. There were still 40,000 Jews living in Bialystok, like a small island in the sea. Many of the Jews were refugees from large and small cities. 20,000 Jews have already disappeared, but in the conditions we live in, it means that Bialystok is still untouched .... The first great wave of extermination occurs on February 5, 1943, when 12,000 Jews are deported to Treblinka and 3,000 are shot in the streets of the ghetto. 200 children suffocated by their own relatives

Page 57

in the hiding places. Many have their hands and feet frozen off. A few dozen are lynched by Jews themselves - as denunciators of their own people.

[The extermination] gets a name. I don't know where this name comes from: "The First Action"—a name that says nothing.

The First "Action" in Bialystok

From February 5 to 14, 1943, Bialystok experienced a bloody eight days. What happened is impossible to describe, either on paper or verbally. I, who saw and witnessed it all, do not understand it to this day: how could this happen? How could "people" (there is no other word to describe those who, at least outwardly, have a human form) take old people, gray-haired people and infants with such cold-bloodedness and sadism and murder them as if it were quite normal and not extraordinary? No one will ever know exactly what happened, because no one is able to describe it in such a way that the reader gets a real picture of it.

On February 1, once again the ghetto was sealed off, no one was allowed out or in. German commissions no longer come to inspect the factories, but only the fences and gates to see if there are any openings. Even the Judenrat walks around agitated. The Germans are handing out potatoes. Whole carloads of potatoes come and are sold for coupons. This is somewhat unusual, because previously one used to get nothing at all except 10 grams of bread for two days. It seems like giving a chicken water to make it easier to pluck.

All the Jews are preparing better hiding places. It is clear to everyone that now it is Bialystok's turn. The underground organization distributes small bottles of vitriol oil [sulfuric acid] in all the factories and prepares the plan

Page 58

of resistance. Various rumors are going around. Some say that the Judenrat is negotiating the extradition of 5,000 Jews in order - as always - to calm the situation. Others say that even the Jewish police, who cooperated with the German, will oppose the extermination.

Before the five days, one simply goes crazy from the many considerations and mental exhaustion. Every evening guards are posted to let people know in case the Germans are coming.

On the night of February 5, when it is not our turn but our neighbor's to keep watch, I come home exhausted from our friend Moti [and his family], whose hiding place I have finished building, and I tiredly fall asleep. While sleeping, I hear people knocking on the shutters and calling out: "Jews, out of the houses! Everyone into the streets!" It is the Jewish police who are shouting.

Our neighbor comes running in, deathly pale, and stammers, barely intelligible: "*Ge-ge-germans are h-h-here!*" Individual shots can be heard in the distance.

I quickly wake up everyone in the house, put on the boots and a jacket (I can't find my pants anymore), quickly send the family to the prepared cellar and crawl into the attic myself with Leybl and neighbors. Not everyone fit into the cellar. After everything was arranged for my parents, I still try to get to the meeting places that had been designated by the underground organization for fighting. But, too late! The streets are blocked by Germans; if anyone shows himself, he is either shot at or seized and put in line with those who will be deported. I have no choice but to go to the attic, where ten people and a small child lie entangled.

Barash's Philosophy

The population's hope in the Jewish police faded away, because they helped the Germans. Barash, as usual,

Page 59

had prepared a paper on which were written the names of the Jews who were to be extradited. A few hours earlier he had summoned the Jewish police with their commander Markus and made a speech in front of them. He said that if a person had a dangerous poisoning and they had to take off a hand to keep him alive, they had to do it. In this way, he wanted to convince them to support the German's work; he thus guaranteed the lives of them and their families.

But the Jews who were on Barash's note could not be found. All were in hiding, except for a group of Jews from other towns who lived in a Synagogue on "Nay-Velt" [Nowy Świat] and had no place to hide. It upset the Germans who were demanding a lot of Jewish blood for their thirsty souls. The commander tore up the paper and began to search all the houses. The first to go is a Jewish policeman, usually holding a hoe or a hammer. After him follows a Ukrainian or White Russian with a gun. Only last to go are the Germans, with guns and hand grenades. They walk slowly and patiently through all the courtyards, smashing the walls, floors and roofs; and while the Ukrainians and the Jewish police do the breaking up, the Germans just watch. If someone is dragged out of his hideout, he is shot or taken to the assembly point on Yurovetske [Jurowiecka] Street, where groups of people are already being collected. In the meantime they are beaten, and dogs tear pieces of them. The Germans are mocking the women, children and old, graying Jews who are standing hungry, frightened and helpless in the frost, betrayed by everyone and abandoned even by God. The greatest cynicism, however, is committed by the Judenrat, which hands out a small loaf of bread to everyone who is taken away. This is to mean that they will be led to work, but they all know that they will eat it in the afterlife, where there might be a lack of provision in view of the arrival of so many people....

The bread must be accepted, and groups of people, huddled because of the cold, go to the gate at Fabritshne [Fabryczna] Street with a loaf of bread under their arms.

Page 60

From time to time the Germans who accompany them fire a shot, and then a Jew rolls into the gutter along with his loaf of bread. The bread, from which the person has just eaten, soaks up with human blood, which runs out of his head....

In the Attic

The first two days I lie with Beybe in the attic, and the parents in the cellar. There is a heavy frost and the wind blows through the cracks in the thin attic walls and the roof tiles. The wind howls as if crying.

Ten of us lie with a small child, one squeezed on top of the other, our feet twisted without being able to straighten them. We have pulled our jackets over our heads to warm ourselves a little with our breath, which is let out slowly so that, God forbid, no noise is made. If someone wants to stretch out his trapped hand, the others give him a nasty look. If you want to relieve yourself, you have to leave it underneath you.

We constantly hear screams and shots of the approaching Germans. Downstairs from us, the door is already being torn open. The child on the mother's lap starts to cry. We are all shaken, what to do? A neighbor puts his hand on the child's mouth. The child is silent, but- forever. As the Germans move away and several shots are heard from them, of which certainly several young lives have fallen in the street, the mother begins to shake her child. But- no voice. The mother begins to scream. It is understandable, but her mouth is held shut, after all, ten people are in danger. The mother cannot calm down and from time to time she utters a great cry of pain that holes our hearts like a bullet.

In the night, after two days, we send someone down to check what's going on. The night is quiet, and it is impossible

Page 61

to remain lying down with a dead child. The messenger reports that we can go down because the Germans use to leave at night. The latter behave like on a normal working day, they come early in the morning at 6, take a two-hour break at noon and leave at 6 in the evening.

In the night we go out. I push myself out of the attic and try to get up to go downstairs, but I fall over. My feet are swollen and frozen off. My brother picks me up in his arms and carries me downstairs to the room. There, everything on the ground is jumbled, the bedding is trampled and torn by German bayonets, a board of the floor is hacked to pieces, that's where the Germans were searching.

Beybe lays me on the bed and cuts open my boots so he can take them off. He goes to check on the parents. Mama with Raytsele come in, wrapped in many rags so as not to freeze to death in the cold. Their lips are parched, their noses and eyes red. My father also drags himself in. We don't talk. Everyone just looks at my swollen feet. My mother takes off her headscarf with a sigh and wraps my feet with it. She asks me if I want something to eat, she is hungry herself but worries about me, goes to the cupboard, but everything is robbed, nothing is left.

Sporadically, people crawl past on the street, like shadows on a wall, bent over and huddled together. One is already missing the whole family or a member of the family, others recognize sisters, brothers, mothers, fathers and children lying shot in the street. There's nothing to hear but convulsions.

The Harmful Division

We learn that the firemen, the burial society, the bakers and the wagoners, who go around with carts to pick up the shot in the streets, are free to move about during the time of their activity. Those who entered the hospital of the ghetto and the factories,

Page 62

are also not harmed for the time being. When the Germans leave, people scramble to go to the factories or, pretending to be sick, to hospitals. But the factories are full, no one new is allowed in, you only get a certificate that you have worked there before, if you have connections. Some push their way in without a certificate and hide in the factory. But the workers look for these people and drive them out into the street. All three shifts sit in the factories, watch their relatives being brought out and shot before their eyes, and they can't help at all. They must continue to sit there and work because "the German" wants it that way and the brigade leaders also demand that they work, because otherwise "the German" comes and leads [the workers] out. Even now the German does not forget the factories and comes from time to time to check if work is being done and if there are any Jews there without a certificate. The families of the policemen also sit in the factories with newly issued certificates. "Their men" bring them food from robbed stores. The others sit there hungry for a whole eight days. But, who can eat in such a time, observing everything through the window?

When the Germans threw away Barash's paper and set out to search themselves, families of the Judenrat were also affected, lying in their hiding places and being discovered. But on the third and fourth day of the extermination, the Judenrat reoriented itself and began again to constantly extradite those with whom it saw fit. At the train station, where usually the Jews were exposed to get into the wagons to be deported to Treblinka, there came such people from the Judenrat who pointed to certain persons to be brought back to the ghetto. All this during the time when people were forcibly herded into the wagons, old mothers were separated from their children and men from their wives, when voices could be heard saying last farewells and consolations, and tears were mixed with the blood of received blows.

Page 63

At the same time, such a person from the Judenrat comes along, whispers something in the ear and promptly someone is led out of the center back to the ghetto. This led to a great demoralization, because every man's life is dear to him after all, and the Germans knew how to take advantage of that by creating a split between the Jews. The latter fell for an [evil] trick. Since it was difficult to find the hidden Jews and the search took too much time, they used to claim, when they found a group in their hiding places, that whoever revealed hiding places of other Jews would go free. Observing that there were Jewish policemen at the side [of the Germans], that nothing happened to the Jews in the factories, and that others were still being taken out of the wagons, not all of them could resist the temptation, and, even if it was only a small part, they broke and agreed to reveal the hiding places. Many of the secret hiding places were revealed in this way, and much damage was done as a result. The Germans, with great cynicism, issued a certificate that the Jew [who had revealed a hiding place] was a traitor and therefore free to roam.

The next morning dawns, we have to go further into hiding. I can't stay in the same place anymore, because I can't watch the mother in her suffering, can't bear how she cradles her dead child and doesn't want to give it out of her hand. It is also too narrow to lie there because I have to lie straight down with my frozen feet and there is no way to stretch out there. My parents and my sister crawl back into their living grave, my brother Leybl takes me in his arms, because I cannot walk, and carries me to another place opposite our yard, to an attic. He puts various bowls and benches in front of our place, so that you can't see that there are people lying there. There are only a few people, so I can lie down stretched out.

Page 64

The Former Bialystok

Bialystok City Garden and the "Imperial Palace" [Branicki Palace]

The railroad station that connected Bialystok with the "big world" and from where the Jews were later deported to Treblinka

Page 65

The Devastated Bialystok

Ovnet's Street, on the right was once the bakery

A note by Dr. Tomek Wisniewski:
"On the corner of Rynek Kościuszki and Zamenhofa Street was a short fragment of street, nicknamed Awnet street (but its official name was Zamenhofa Street)—Awnet was the owner of a famous short grocery and bakery."
https://www.jewishbialystok.pl/T._Aron_Awnet,5400,4869

The place where the Bialystok Synagogue stood. The whole Synagogue yard and the surrounding streets are as if wiped away.

Page 66

What I Saw with my Own Eyes

The fourth day is sunny and there is a heavy frost. The ghetto is quiet. The only sounds we hear are groans from the "third street" and shouting from the Germans. Through a crack in the wall, a frosty wind blows, cutting through the body more than anything else today, I see Bialostotshanske [Białostoczańska] Street and a piece of Polna Street. Specifically, I observe our courtyard, where my parents and Raytsele are lying. I see Jewish police, Germans, Ukrainians and Belorussians who are serving in the German military, walking around and searching. Silence in the ghetto, everyone lies there in fear. The pavement is strewn with food and coats, with dead Jews, children, not yet cleared away in the few days, in various poses, stiffened and frozen, with a trickle of blood next to each one. Individual groups of detected Jews, huddled together, difficult to recognize, are led by the Germans. An elderly woman stays a little behind, she cannot follow. The German calls out: "Come, come!" She falls on the pavement from weakness, the German points his rifle at her, one shot, and a pool of blood is running from her head. She stopped moving and died instantly. The daughter, who had hooked her mother under as she walked, stops beside the dead body and mutters to herself: "A-a-already o-o-over!" The German, completely calm, calls to her: "Come, come, come!" The daughter starts to walk, another shot is fired and she rolls into the gutter, 10 meters in front of her mother. She picks herself up several more times, shouting unclear words. The group continues walking, huddled together, as if nothing happened. A young man trying to escape is also shot; the German laughs when he sees that the bullet did not kill him right away. And further silence in the ghetto.

Another group of Germans begins to search further. They enter the yard where I had lain before. It does not take long and they find the place where I was hidden the day before; and now

Page 67

people are brought out from there. I recognized them because of the dead child the mother is carrying in her arms. A small tangle of people is moving, the mother with the dead child in front, next to her her husband and two older daughters holding on to their parents' rags. This time the child did not scream and betray the hiding place. They purposely put the child in the front so that those who come to search would think that they had already been there because there was a dead child there. But, it was a mistake. When the Germans saw that the child had no injury from a weapon, they knew that it was not the work of the Germans and began to search vigorously until they actually found the hiding place. They shot two people immediately. The rest I saw being brought out. If my brother hadn't carried me over, I with my frozen feet would have been among them, and they would certainly have shot me.

Malmed

I lay there, watching what was happening, realizing how pointless it was to hide when everyone was looking for you, and I had sick feet to boot. Out of 50 thousand people crammed along several streets, only one person in the ghetto used vitriol [sulfuric acid] and cold weapons [knives, etc.], which everyone had taken with him to his hiding place. There were no more vigorous people. This was the most terrible thing about the process of annihilation, until one heroic Jew, Malmed, a refugee from Slonim, who had realized earlier that there was no other way out than to fight death, set a great example. Malmed had joined the partisans from Slonim, but the German, with the help of Lithuanian and Latvian divisions, forced the partisans to retreat due to heavy losses. He then arrived in Bialystok, where after a short time he witnessed the extermination process. Immediately he realized the nonsense

Page 68

of hiding, so he stayed at home and waited. The first to come in was a Jewish policeman who tried to herd him out into the street to the Germans. He did nothing to him. When the Germans saw that nothing happened to the Jewish policeman, a German also entered the apartment. Malmed immediately stood up to him, poured sulfuric acid on his face, which burned his face and blinded him. Then he fled. This happened on Kupyetske [Kupiecka] Street 10.

Immediately the Germans issued a decree to shoot the first 200 Jews who were in the same place. They were shot in Prage's garden, on Nayvelt [New World, Nowy Świat]. It was announced that immediately all Jews in the place will be shot if Malmed is not brought. I cannot clarify with certainty whether the Jewish police found him and handed him over or whether he reported on his own so as not to bring harm to the ghetto. On Kupyetske [Kupiecka] Street a gallows was erected on which he was hanged together with his wife (they thus saved themselves from taking her to Treblinka). This Malmed was the only hero within the eight days. **Honor to his memory and be it a moral lesson for the survivors!** After the "liquidation" comrades hid him in the cemetery of the ghetto and erected a monument with his picture and the picture of his wife.

There were also cases of passive resistance. When a group was found in their hiding place, some shouted out specially: "Against the old Jews, against weak women and infants you won the war, but you will not take Stalingrad! Down with Hitler!" After such an exclamation, these Jews, of course, were shot on the spot. Thus, they avoided further torment. After all, it was like this: if you asked the Germans to shoot, they remained "polite" and answered with "no".

On the Way to Treblinka

The searches continue. They are still looking for the "great enemies"

Page 69

of humanity, the Jewish babies, old people and women. Next to us, where we are lying hidden, many people are found today in their hideouts. Many also lie shot in the yards, in the streets, in the attics and houses. The people from the Jewish burial society with their green hats and dead faces pile the dead on carts, one on top of the other, like wooden boxes. While they take some to the cemetery on Zhabya [Żabia, Frog] Street, they lay out other bodies in a row because there is no time to bury them all. Those who remain alive are taken to Poleske [Poleska] Street, herded into the wagons, and then the doors are locked. Four Germans sit on top of each wagon with machine guns and shoot at anyone who tries to escape. However, many jump out just when the train is moving fastest, tearing open the windows and doors. Many dead bodies of young boys and girls remained on the way to Treblinka. Those who managed to save themselves wandered around hungry, unable to return to the ghetto because it was guarded. Many of them were seized by the Poles, robbed if they had anything, and handed over to the Germans. Others roamed the woods for weeks, trying to link up with partisans.

In those days, Jews met their deaths in different ways. There were cases of parents who came out of hiding because of their screaming child and surrendered, sacrificing themselves for their child. Many took their own lives; others lost their minds. Very many human and inhuman acts could be seen in those critical eight days of terrible extermination.

How was it possible to lie there, see such indescribable and unbelievable cases of how people treated other people, and remain silent? I can't understand it myself. I don't feel now, as I write this, what we felt then, and I don't know how it was possible to look each other in the eye, without reacting to it, not

Page 70

rebelling against it the slightest bit. What kind of creature is the man who can lie in hiding, watching something like this and waiting until he too is found soon?

After the Storm

Finally, isolated Jews can be seen again, crawling out and hastening through the streets. One makes sure that the Germans are no longer coming, although the ghetto is still sealed off everywhere. Beybe picks me up in his arms and carries me down to the apartment. Everything there is robbed and jumbled. I lie down in bed, my frozen feet hurt a lot. A doctor is called who orders that I get injections, which are very expensive. My mother is sitting next to my bed, she is afraid that I will faint from pain.

All the friends of our family were taken away, only we remained. The commotion that remained within the population must get discharged. Whole families were wiped out, which had woven their lives here for generations. The Judenrat perceives and understands the mood in the ghetto. To divert the anger that would be discharged on him, they take three young boys, arrest them, reporting that they, the three boys, in the time of the extermination, took boots and finger rings from shot Jews and robbed the apartments. The population tears itself to the mother to lynch her. The Judenrat sentences the boys to death and actually hangs them opposite the Judenrat. Whether the accusations were true or it was just three more victims of the Judenrat, I don't know for sure. But, the Jewish police [definitely] robbed. I saw that myself in those days, and with the condemnation they took the attention away from themselves.

As soon as we came out of our holes into the "bright world," it was enough for someone on the street to shout that a special person was a denunciator, and all the Jews of the street fell upon him, lynching him

Page 71

on the spot. Every day, several people were lynched in this way. It also happened that Jews went to the apartment of such an informer and stabbed him with a knife.

But life goes on, those who stayed have to go on living. The hospital is full of people with frostbite, where parts of the body have to be amputated: Hands, feet and ears. Many remain cripples. I lie in the parlor, tossing and turning in pain. My feet have to be amputated, but there is no room in the hospital. The doctor gives me injections and after a week of treatment he assures me that my feet will be preserved.

Life in the ghetto is even more difficult than before. For a few more weeks the ghetto remains closed, and the only food is a plate of soup that you get from a kitchen. Later, when you are allowed to work outside the ghetto again, you are led like a prisoner, accompanied by a guard. At work, one is also guarded with weapons. The inflation is extraordinary: a loaf of bread costs 100 marks and a pood of potatoes 300 marks. The "great salvation " is the little bit of soup that is given out around 12 o'clock.

The Split of the Underground Organization

After the week of liquidation of February 5, 1943, and the failure of the "Samooborone" (self-defense), the youth of the underground organization demanded to focus on arming and fighting in the forest. The older part of the organization tried to refute this idea by explaining that the forest could not accommodate so many people, and in the ghetto would remain elderly people and children who would have to be defended. In her opinion, the defense needed to be improved with regard to a recurrence.

Page 72

One comrade, Yeudite (1), vehemently defended the youth's point of view, and at three meetings it was pointed out that the reason why "the forest" could not only achieve little by February 5, but on the contrary there were many victims, was because there were far too few weapons. Therefore, it was necessary to send more people and weapons and to seek contact with other forests where more Russian partisans were staying.

However, not everyone agreed with this, and it came to a split. The movement "Yeudite" divided from the organization with a group of young people and began to take action on its own initiative. I joined the Yeudite group and we began to work feverishly for our new path. The older comrades of the former organization even tried to block us by means of various slanders, but they did not succeed. The organization was spreading very much.

In the forests around Bialystok, where it was decided to create the base of our partisan group, there were already very small partisan groups, most of them consisting of escaped Russian prisoners of war and individual Jews from the province, which had long been liquidated. The work of the Russian partisan groups consisted of various disruptive actions: Blowing trains off the tracks, shooting Polish agents who collaborated with the Germans, and so on. We initiated a contact with such a group, whose leader was "Afronasitsh". From him we asked for support, guidance and help to teach us comrades how to keep ourselves in the forest. Our first comrades who went to the forest did not yet

----

*(1)   **author's note:** Her real name is not known. She came from Warsaw and was one of the first to organize the resistance movement in Bialystok. She fell during the uprising, on September 16, 1944, in the Bialystok ghetto.*

[***translator's note:*** It can be assumed that her name was Yudita Vogrudska (Judith Nowogrodzka), see Forverts, page 7
https://www.nli.org.il/en/newspapers/frw/1958/02/04/01/article/48/?srpos=8&e=-------en-20--1--img-txIN%7ctxTI-
%d7%99%d7%a6%d7%97%d7%a7+%d7%9e%d7%90%d6%b7%d7%9c%d7%9e%d7%a2%d7%93-------------1]

and see https://jewishcurrents.org/may-24-judith-nowogrodzka-bialystok-ghetto

Page 73

understand how to get food with weapons but risked their lives to go from the forest to the ghetto to buy food for money (!). This brought many difficulties and days of starvation.

Afronasitshe's group accepted us and taught the comrades to cope with weapons as well as that food was not to be bought for money. So it really happened; I went to the forest with sixty marks and came back from the war with this money.

Weapons Are Stocked Up and People Are Sent into the Woods

In the ghetto, the organization decided at meetings to get even more weapons to send to the forest. So they instructed every comrade, whatever he was working on, that he would have to bring parts of weapons. It was also decided to carry out thefts at night in the factories of the ghetto, where German uniforms had been worked out. We usually carried these uniforms to the Russian groups in the forest, for which they gave us weapons. We also assembled radios and carried them into the forest. So it happened that for one radio and a few German costumes we suddenly got a machine gun and eight rifles. On this basis, we were already able to send many comrades into the forest.

Our group increased in size and we asked a commander to lead us. We went mainly under a Russian commander who accompanied us on destruction work and taught us to keep contact with the Russian groups. We also met a very energetic Russian group named after their leader, Groza. The forest [movement] developed a "very interesting life story" that relied heavily on help from the ghetto.

Page 74

In the ghetto, every comrade who was designated to go out into the woods had to pass a preparation, because many comrades did not know how to handle a rifle. In a room on Tshiste [Czysta] Street, the selected comrades met to prepare. Benches were set up and they practiced hitting a target on them. Especially popular was a rifle, with which one lay on the floor and had to complete certain exercises. We also assembled bombs in the ghetto. Once, on a beautiful day, the ghetto was shaken by a strong explosion on Tshiste [Czysta] Sreet 8, where three of our comrades were making a bomb. The three comrades were blown to pieces. A German commission came, and it was said that the Judenrat covered up the matter. It was explained in such a way that an oven had exploded in the bakery, which was downstairs in the building.

At that time, a denunciator who worked in the Gestapo was also stabbed to death. He still lived in the hospital for several days and received sick visits from his comrades. The organization took advantage of that; two armed comrades came out of the forest and waited. When one of the informers came out of the hospital, they shot him. (By a coincidence, a stranger was also shot.) Thus "the forest" cooperated with the ghetto.

———

It was not allowed to bring food [from the ghetto] into the forest. The comrades learned to get food themselves from the surrounding population with the help of weapons. The latter, however, was informed at the same time that our struggle was also a struggle for their own liberation. The population identified with us, helped us a lot and informed us about the position and number of Germans. They did not withdraw their sympathy from us. From our side we shot at the agents of the area who caused suffering to the population and to us.

Page 75

In our activity, we always had to go through certain experiences. Once 10 men (from the ghetto) were sent out into the forest with weapons. In the night they crawled over the fence and wanted to cross the railroad tracks near the "Bialystotshek" [Bialystoczek] (1). Five of them got across, but the other five failed to do so, because a train was just coming up. In the meantime, a German patrol arrived, noticed them and shouted, "Stop!" Comrade [Shimon] Datner immediately shot at them, wounding one. This set off an alarm, but the shooting stopped, and several days later (they all) returned to the ghetto. Everyone dug his gun into a different designated place. [Given this incident] a rumor spread in the ghetto that partisans wanted to tear their way into the ghetto, a real sensation. We learned from these mistakes. Instead of climbing over the fence, we removed quite a few boards and put them back in position so that it would not be noticed. Next, there was an even greater relief for the comrades who were sent into the forest. They usually took their weapons with them and were taken with the help of comrade Zalman Finkel, who brought carts of dung from the ghetto to the villages, where he additionally hid things and led them out. This is how the youth fought.

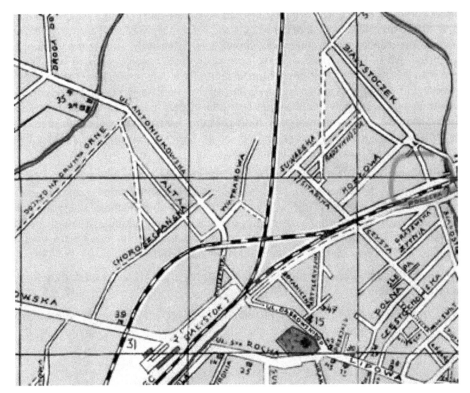

(1) [On the map you can see the intersection of the former Bialystoczek Street with the railroad line, photo: Dr. Tomek Wisniewski]

I Save Myself from the Executioner's Hands

The constant arrests do not stop, and since our family is not spared any misfortune, one particular night I am actually arrested as well. A Jewish policeman pulls me out of bed and leads me away to the "Sing-Sing", as they called the prison where the detainees in the ghetto were held. I learn that in the Agustov [Augustów] camp they need three painters for work; next to me, two other painters are already sitting under the bars, waiting for us to be handed over to the Gestapo. Mom comes to the bars in tears

Page 76

and asks, what should we do? Beybe wants to change places with me, to go to prison for me, but I don't want that. I comfort my mother and turn around the room, back and forth, looking at the inscriptions on the walls of people who have been there and were sent away to various camps, many of whom are no longer alive.

The Jewish police chases my mother away, a Gestapo vehicle drives up, from which a coarse German with a black hat, on which is a skull, gets out. He yells at the policemen who prance around him. The door is locked and we go into the vehicle. Mother stands on a street corner, eyes swollen, wringing her hands. We are taken to the Gestapo building, where we are ordered to get out of the vehicle and wait. In the Gestapo courtyard there are many people standing, with their faces turned to a brick wall, so that they cannot be recognized. All of them, however, have been badly beaten, some smeared with blood, some with bandages. One falls down from standing for a long time. The person watching over him with a rifle goes to him and beats him all over until he gets up and stands against the wall again. Every now and then you hear a heartbreaking scream of someone being tortured somewhere in a room of the building. In the courtyard, people are turning back and forth, working there as if nothing is happening. They've been working there for three years now and they have been seeing it every day.

"What can be done?", I think. Now I have been standing here for an hour, and what will they do with me? Meanwhile, I observe that a German with a rifle is standing next to the gate, not checking any of the workers who go out with their tools. I tear down the yellow patches, take a brush that is lying in the yard and start talking to a Jewish worker who goes out to the gate to work; I accompany him, talking to him as if I were working with him. The German standing by the gate lets us through.

After we have walked a bit, I tell the Jew to take the brush [1] and head straight for the forest. Out of habit

[1] *translator's note*: literally "bretl, small bord", but I think that the "bershtl", the brush he carried, is what is meant

Page 77

I walk on the cobblestones, but soon I remember that, without patches, I have to walk on the sidewalk. Looking around like a rabbit, I go home, towards the ghetto. I crawl over the fence of the yard where I was working and come inside to a couple of Jewish upholsterers working in a special room. They immediately understand that I have fled and hide me under the pile of mattresses lying there. It is known in the ghetto that I have been arrested and the Germans must not see me. The Jews hide me well and provide me with food; they decide that I should enter the ghetto together with them, but we will be one too many! Thereupon a comrade of mine risks his life, takes the way over the fence and bribes the German with several marks so that he keeps silent. I pull my cap over my eyes, change my clothes with those of the comrade and go into the ghetto. During the night I sleep at the home of a comrade and during the day I go to another place. In this way I hide for two days. Raytsele brings me food from home.

Our New Comrade—the Rifle

I realize that it is nonsensical to continue hiding and I contact the organization that now, given my situation, I would like my turn to be sent to the forest. Acknowledging this, on the day of August 12, they inform me to go to a meeting point. There a comrade will come and take me to a place from which I will get to the partisan group.

Evening falls and it becomes dark. I sneak through the little bit of street and go home to say goodbye. Beybe goes out into the street and watches to make sure no one is there either. I explain to my mother that I couldn't earn anything for the family anyway, since they are looking for me, and that I have to go to the forest. She turns pale and does not answer. It becomes quiet in the parlor. I go to my father, who is lying in bed, and we hug and kiss. Mother is still standing in the same place, silent.

Page 78

I hug her and a warm tear falls on my cheek. She whispers, "Be blessed and happy!" Raytsele walks out of the parlor. I leave money and food for two weeks, take my "burke" (short winter jacket) and leave. Beybe accompanies me to the house where I have to go in, he is not allowed in there.

Ten men are already sitting in the parlor. All are silent and look at each other. Two comrades who came from the "forest" for bandages and other things talk about the "forest" and about the preparation of the new people in the coming week. It can be felt that people from the "forest" are already somewhat different people, they have quite different concerns in life.

The female comrades eagerly try to fill our backpacks, they pour water into canteens [menażkas]. Several rifles are brought in, and late at night we slowly crawl, two by two, to the fence. One of the fence slats is opened and silently, not even breathing, we walk out. The first regulation is called: Shoot immediately if you come across a German or policeman who could hinder us. We go out one after the other and passing through Bialostotshek [Bialostoczek] we come to the road to Knishiner [Knyszyn] forest, our first target point.

The night is silent, we go with the guns, ready to fight at any minute. There is already a different smell in the air, you feel more human and get a little human dignity, you go without patches, free! Your best comrade is the rifle that never betrays you. But also we must not betray our comrade rifle; until the last bullet - the last bullet is for you - this is what demands from us the new morality, the common agreement that must bring the victory!

At dawn we reach a point where earlier, on a small mountain, there was a camp. Now there is a pit, everything is jumbled and destroyed by shells. Our guide tells us: "Two weeks ago, our group was attacked, fought with the Germans, and we had to mourn one victim, our comrade Fishl. A few dozen meters

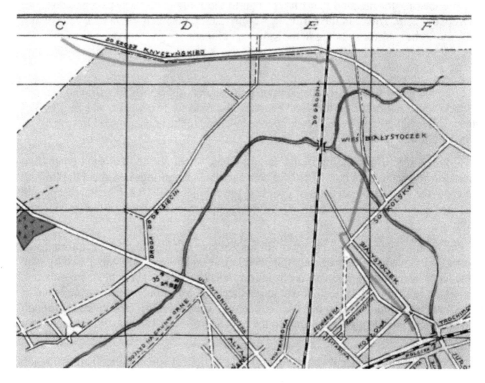

[The way to the woods of Knyszyn, from a photo of Dr. Tomek Wisniewski]

Page 79

away is Fishl's grave, a freshly heaped up mound. We stand around the grave and each of us is engrossed in our thoughts. With our gazes we say goodbye to the grave and make our way to a new point where our comrades are located.

It is not until daybreak that we arrive there. A comrade standing guard there welcomes us with a smile, quietly squeezes each one's hand and kisses them. He inquires about the situation in the ghetto. A small fire burns between trees, two cauldrons hang on a stick, in which food is cooking, prepared especially for us. They knew that two new comrades were arriving today.

We sit down around the fire, drying ourselves from the morning dampness that has soaked our clothes. We get to eat a thick porridge with a lot of meat; for a long time we have not eaten meat! We are told that today comrade Khayim Khalef will come with the commander of the other forests, who have conducted secret negotiations with a group of the same ghetto, which is now in the Suprasler [Supraśl] forest. We are shown the place, not far from the fire, where we must go to sleep, undressed, with the rifle in our hands. From now on we have to be ready to fight every minute, because we don't know when the German can meet us.

But, we are not asleep. There is so much to think about. The comrades who have been in the forest for a while are discussing internal matters, we can't get a word in edgewise yet because it's a completely different language. They reassure us about the various sounds that can be heard in the forest from time to time, they say that it doesn't mean anything and that we will soon get used to it and later be able to distinguish what it is.

The next morning the commander arrives, a young Russian with a good-natured and cheerful face. He greets each one separately, sits among us and asks various things; at the same time he tells the news he has brought from the other forests. He informs us that a federation is now being formed of all the groups

Page 80

that are in the forests. A union will be established, and all the groups will be concentrated in certain places in the Suprasler [Supraśl] Forest and its surroundings. We too have to go there and, according to the orders of the staff, we are placed in a certain section so that they know where we are and can send us commands.

We are preparing to leave. Everyone who has served in the military is assigned the more important weapons. I get the machine gun, weighing 16 kilos and loaded with 63 bullets per magazine that it can fire at one time.... The machine gun is called "Donskoy", after its former owner, a Don Cossack. They give me two additional magazines with 124 bullets and instruct me on how to handle the machine gun, because I have only known different models before. As soon as the night falls, we prepare for the first "Bombyazhke" (*), then leave this forest and go over to the Suprasler [Supraśl] forest...

The Uprising in the Bialystok Ghetto
(the last extermination of the remaining 40 thousand Jews)

When the uprising in the ghetto began on August 16, 1943, I was no longer there. Four days earlier I was sent to the forest, where we stood at our posts to pick up the fighting comrades and Jews who ran into the forest. From them I learned exactly what happened and in what way the uprising was stifled.

During the last period, the underground organizations had been working even more intensively and they began to talk about broadening the work by uniting more organizations into one

---

(*) **author's note**: "Bombyazhke" was the name the partisans used to give to encircling a village with weapons at night, taking necessary food and clothes.

Page 81

force. Under the pressure of the "forest", the so-called "Yehudim [Yeudite?] Group" was united with the old organization and the (Ha)Chalutz [Pioneer] groups were also to be included in the cooperation. Barash, too, had reoriented and looked for the leaders of the organization. He partially supported the Zionist Chalutz movement with money, but he knew that this was not the right force to rely on and tried to talk

A tragic picture: the medical staff of the Bialystok Hospital is led out on the way to Treblinka.

to the Polish organization. However, the Germans worked much faster....

Early in the morning of August 16, the ghetto was suddenly surrounded, the Judenrat was occupied and it was reported that all Jews

Page 82

were being led out to work (the "old song"). Everyone knew very well what this meant, because even children and aged people were called "to work". The organizations immediately took positions on the agreed places, on Tsheple [Ciepła] Street, Novogrudzke [Novogrodzka] and Khmielne [Chmielna] Street. Weapons were distributed and it was decided to start the fight by firing at the fence, which was surrounded by Germans, and, taking many Jews along, to break through into the forest. Quite a few factories were set on fire and there was heavy shooting in the courtyards and houses at the Germans, who patrolled the ghetto and threw grenades at the fence to break through. Many Germans fell and the rest retreated.

Realizing the attitude of the fighters—the fight lasted already half a day—the Germans brought several tanks into the ghetto, dividing the streets and cutting off the connections between the groups. They also reinforced the guard around the fence, and it was impossible to break through. The comrades fought for a whole day. Not having any connection with the leaders and not knowing what to do further, the groups became more and more thinned, many comrades had fallen. The rest fought by setting fire to the houses that had to be abandoned.

It proved to be extremely counterproductive that the grenades, which had been manufactured in the ghetto, did not explode, because they had been lying in a damp place all the time.

At dawn, our brother Leybl (Beybe), as a disciplined member of the organization, immediately put himself forward to fight. Leaving his home, he immediately gets weapons and fights on the position designated for him in Novogrudzke [Novogrodzka] Street. During an attack he is wounded in his hand; he does not leave his fighting place but continues fighting wounded until the evening. Later they learn that they should mask and go to stand with the other Jews

Page 83

at the train station, and then jump off the train and head for the forest. Together with several comrades who bandage his wound, they rush over to the mass of people who are led in rows to the train and later, when they are already on the train, they tear open a board and jump out after the Lape [Łapy] station. He manages to reach the forest, unfortunately, not where I and the others were, but in the woods of Breynsk [Brańsk]. There were no partisans there yet. The four of them live there without a gun, obtaining food

Beybe, perished at the age of twenty two.

in various ways. This is what those who were with him told me. During this time his hand heals, and so they remain there until winter. In winter, however, the Poles learned from the still visible traces of the comrades where they were hiding, and there was a danger that they would come and murder them. Therefore, they decide to leave the place and divide into groups of two men each.

Page 84

From then on, there is no more news of Beybe and his comrade. The other two remained alive. I spoke with one of them. Thus ends Beybe's 22 years young life. Nevertheless, his attitude and dignified human spirit should be a consolation for us. He fought as a wounded man and did not lose his courage. Honor his memory, our pride for us as brothers and children of the [Jewish] people!

The Cruel End

The struggle of the Jewish population was immediately crushed in the first few days. The Germans still tried to deceive the Jews and divided them, saying that a smaller ghetto would remain. They segregated a certain number of Jews on Fabritshne [Fabryczna] Street, where they were supposedly allowed to continue living, and exploited them by having them clean up the factories and take out the machines; after that, they too were killed.

Thousands were shot in the city, on the streets of the ghetto and while being led away over the roads outside the ghetto. Next to the railroad they rounded up all the women, children and men and kept them for days without food and drink, until people began to have fits of weakness and asked themselves to be led to the wagons, because that would ultimately be a "salvation". The last extermination action was one hundred percent more cruel than the first one of February 5 of the same year, and it is impossible to even begin to describe it. Many people hid in the hiding places they had prepared, but gradually they were discovered by the Germans. Throughout the year, when the ghetto was closed, until the entering of the Red Army, groups with Germans and Polish workers were sent to clean up the houses and bring out everything that remained inside. When they came across such hiding places of Jews who were half dead from lying crammed together for months without being able to change their clothes, wash or comb their hair,

Page 85

and who could live only on dry food, the Germans used to gather them in groups, deport them south of the city to Pyetrashe [Pietrasze] or Novoshilki [Nowosiółki], dig pits and shoot them there naked. One of the Jews, Aberzinski, managed to escape from such a "living pit". He came to us in the forest and told us everything. We took in many Jews in the forest, gave them a new home and weapons, with the possibility of taking revenge on those who did that to us.

This ends my colorless account of the tragedy of over 60 thousand Jews in the Bialystok ghetto. There still remain the descriptions of the struggle and life of the created partisan movement in the forests around Bialystok, which I try to pass on.

My first "Bombyashke"

As soon as it is dark and night falls, the commander has us stand together and tells us how we should behave towards the population when we enter the village; what we can ask for or not. He assigns everyone their tasks and off we go; three comrades, the scouts, go ahead, the rest go one after the other, in a line, silently to the designated place. Through streams and swamps, over paths that have never borne a human foot, we come to the village we can see from afar. We stop, lie down on the ground to listen and wait to see what happens. Quite a few comrades are sent to find out what the situation of this area is, where German patrols are, to scout out the route we have to take and where exactly we have to go. Lying down, we wait for their signs.

The village is noisy with constant sounds. Dogs go at each other, gentile girls go noisily from the field, laughing and shouting. Wagons, loaded with grain, creak slowly forward. Cows walk with udders full of milk

Page 86

that we will drink soon. The comrades come back and signal with their hands that we can enter the village. We go out, surround the village on several paths, set up posts with weapons on the paths that lead to other villages. I, with the submachine gun, take position on the road leading to the town, from which it is thought that Germans may come. The other comrades scatter around the village to collect the food we need for our way.

For the most part, the peasants accommodate us with sympathy, bring milk outside to drink, inquire about news from the front and how life is in the forest. They wait with impatience to be liberated by the Red Army and give us different news concerning the German forces. The comrades quickly bring out the received products to the gathering point, where they are packed to be able to carry them on the way.

Meanwhile, a farmer comes to me and tells me that the ghetto is burning and all the Jews in Bialystok are being shot. (It is only the third day that I am away from there.) I immediately transmit this to the comrades, who don't believe it and answer: "He recognized that you are a Jew, and he says that specifically because he is probably angry that we are taking food away from him." However, we see that the sky around us is red. Not long ago we left the ghetto and we had no idea that such an annihilation was about to happen there.

With our minds already elsewhere, we quickly finish the work and leave the village to go to the Suprasler [Supraśl] forest, where we have been ordered; and with the food and weapons on our shoulders, we leave in deep anxiety. What to do now? We rest and before leaving the Knishin [Knyszyn] forest we fire a volley of shots in memory of our victims, who fell in battle with the Germans.

In the Suprasler [Supraśl] Woods

We walk all night and arrive at dawn in the Suprasler [Supraśl] forest, where we are shown the new place, our new home,

Page 87

new trees and new earth. All day long we have guests in our "new home". Russian groups from the area come to visit us and introduce themselves, and at the same time everyone gets together for a conference to discuss how we can organize our further work in the forests together. It is clear to all of us that while we are talking, our ghetto is being annihilated, where our comrades are fighting who did not manage to get into the forest. Now, we will not receive any contact and support from the ghetto. Also, we must prepare for large raids by the Germans in our forests, because all Jews who manage to break through the ghetto will flee into the forests, knowing that there is a partisan group.

There is a difficult situation in the forests now. All the fleeing Jews come without weapons, making our work more difficult as well. The deliberations take a long time, what should be done now? And how is all this to be organized? The Russian groups express that they want to go east, where there are more military cohorts and larger forests. They decide to leave the forests around Bialystok to gather large forces around them elsewhere and come back. Our opinion and duty is to stay to accommodate our comrades and all the Jews for whom we partisans in the forest are the only salvation.

The Russian groups leave and we remain alone, waiting for our Jewish brothers to take them in and prepare them for further struggle. We arrange with the Russian groups certain contact points when they will come back to us with information. We undertake quite a few "bomyashkes", prepare food for those who will come and post our comrades outside on the paths leading from the city to the forest, so that they can pick up the Jews they meet and bring them to us.

We bring many men and women that we meet straying in all places of the forest, we give them food and assign them temporarily

Page 88

to certain parts of the forest, where we place some comrades with weapons to protect them. A few times a day we bring them food. Several of our comrades are killed by explosions while they are at their post to pick up and seek out the wandering Jews. Many Jews are being shot by Germans who are making large raids in the forests to look for the partisans. We continue our work resolutely, because we have not come to guard our lives in the woods; we have gone out to fight and must take in everyone we meet, whether our forces now will make that possible or not. Finally, after the extermination of the Jews in the ghetto, our base has been destroyed, from which we have received bandages, radios, weapons and people. Thus begins our tragedy in the forest. An influx of Jews without weapons is coming, and we are taking them with us, relying on our own forces.

Jews in the Forest

In the forests there were different groups of Jews. There were private groups, that is, Jews from all the towns that had been liquidated were lying in the forest in groups of 5-10 unarmed people in pits. They bought food for their money from known farmers or exchanged various valuables they still had. When they had no more money or valuables, many of these groups would go out into the fields at harvest time and gather potatoes or other vegetables at night to prepare for winter as best they could. They simply lived with nothing. If we happened to come across such a group, they were like the living dead. When we looked at the people, we couldn't tell which of them was a woman and which was a man, because they were all parched like plants that don't get water.

When we met such groups of Jews, we explained to them that it was important to fight in the forest and not lie there

Page 89

waiting for liberation. We took comrades [from their groups], showed them all the other meeting places in the forest, and also designated people from their midst to maintain ongoing contact with us. Their task now was to procure weapons from the surrounding neighbors from the money they had, and we combined their commission with ours by teaching them how to get food. We accepted them, including them in all the acts of sabotage we carried out. The influx of Jews after the complete liquidation of the ghetto complicated our organizational work and preparations for winter life in the forest. Nevertheless, we took them all in, providing for them according to our means and sharing everything we possessed at that time.

The Contact with the City

We continued our work as a group from Bialystok in contact and with the support of the underground organization P.P.R. [Polish Communist Party], which existed in the city, outside the ghetto, and was composed of former members of the Communist Party.

From our side there remained five comrades: Roze Vyesbitski, under the pseudonym "Marilke", Khaye Grosman and three others, whose names I do not remember. Living outside the ghetto with Aryan passports, they used to come to us in the forest, bringing from the city necessary information, weapons and bandages, when raids took place and we could not go out [of the forest] and move. In the times when we were separated from them and could not, thanks to their help, be in contact with our partisan group, the great feat they accomplished cannot be described and conveyed. I will only

Page 90

mention individual facts of their work that best describe their perseverance and dedication in the fight against Nazi fascism. Every wandering Jew, hiding in various ways, whom they met in the city, when Bialystok was already "Judenrein", they used to take him in, hide him until night and bring him to us at agreed

Khaye Grosman

points in the forest, where we accommodated them. The comrade Rivke Madeyska found a little boy wandering in the city and took him in to bring him to the forest. But the boy had no patience to wait until night and went out to mend his shoes. He walked barefoot through the city.

Page 91

The Gestapo stopped him and, realizing that he was Jewish, forced him to testify by various means where he had been hiding until now, because there were no Jews left in the city. The boy told them where the comrade had hidden him. Immediately a group of Germans ran, surrounded the house and wanted to arrest the comrade. But she, seeing who was knocking at the door, immediately understood what had happened and tried to escape through the window. A German chased after her and wounded her with his dagger. The comrade Rivke Madeyska was wounded. She lay in the hospital for several days before she died, not wanting to reveal a single word, not even that she was Jewish, because she did not want further questioning to endanger her comrades who were carrying on the work.

The comrades also had contact with several Jews who were in prison and organized their escape into the forest. Through them we received bandages, medicine, radios, weapons and people. Thanks to them, comrade Berl Shatsman, a fugitive from prison, also joined us. Their work and the permanent contact with our partisan group facilitated many things, and later, when we met with the Russian groups, they became our most important factor concerning the connection with the city. They even manage to establish a contact with a German, a director of a factory, who brings weapons to the partisans and comes to the forest especially to see partisans.

Our then-commander of the brigade, Vaytshekhovski, welcomed him with a great parade. Today the German is in Moscow as a free citizen.

Our Organizational Difficulties

During the time when we had posted our comrades on all the roads to pick up the wandering Jews in our group,

Page 92

more than 80 Jews were taken in by us, men and women, all of them without weapons, who could only save a single piece of clothing they were wearing on their bodies when they fled. We divided them all into special groups and brought them food. These conditions were very unfamiliar to us; people who had never been in an organization and, in addition, were still in shock over the destruction of the ghetto; they did not understand what our task was. Great difficulties arose in the forest because of them. All our efforts to classify them, our requests to give us money so that we could get weapons or other things, met with problems. They were not prepared to develop understanding for the work in the forest and were mostly selfish, wanting only to improve their own situation without considering the others.

We did not want to force them to take over our duties, and this was actually a mistake on our part. We behaved too democratically, and this brought long weeks of starvation after the arrival of so many Jews. We simply lived with one boiled potato a day, understanding that we had to wait for a certain time. After all, they did not understand all this and tore back to the city to buy food for money, what was impossible in view of the Gestapo raids. One of them even tried to persuade our two comrades to leave in order to get something for the others. They actually fled, at a time when we were in the most difficult situation. This forced us to divide all the Jews into special groups. Some of the private groups were also divided separately; we sent comrades every day to bring them food and protect them. When we got more weapons, we took comrades from them into our fighting group. In the forests further east around Volkovisk, Slonim and Baranovitsh [Baranovichi],

Page 93

conditions were much easier: larger forests, larger groups of partisans, more weapons. There it was usually possible to create zones where for months no German foot could enter. Only in certain times of big battles, when the Germans raised whole divisions to fight, they used to push back the Germans with losses or left the place in time. When escaped Jews encountered such a group, they were safer and more cared for. At the same time, they used to fall under a military discipline right away.

In our forests we could not create such zones because of the large crossings of railroads and main roads. We had to fight much more often, to face the German eye to eye; and we had to be more stubborn in the face of hunger, which was a constant companion. Not all of us could understand and endure this; for this purpose, one had to have been prepared earlier in one's education, and many did lack this, which is why they understood the task in the forest too late. The group, now formed of gunmen, consisted of three "pulemyotn" [machine guns], two "dyesatkes" (a gun that shoots 10 bullets at once), ordinary rifles and a revolver. Those who had weapons were divided by us into the group of armed men, which had to supply all the other groups with everything, and at the same time procure weapons, blow up bridges and railroads, and get rid of various spies and provocateurs. We also had to continue to maintain contact with our female comrades in the city and prepare for winter, which set in early.

The German Raid on our "Dzhelyanke" (*)

Part of our armed group took up their work

(*) *author's note: "dzhelyanke"= that's what we called a part of the forest where one of our groups was located. Each "dzhelyanke" had a number, which served us as an orientation point where a group was positioned.*

Page 94

in another forest. In the Suprasl [Supraśl] forest we stayed with 30 men, armed with two "pulemyotn", one "dyesatke" and the remaining rifles. In special places in the forest sat the unarmed groups with whom we met every day to supply them, and from which we took comrades to all the places of our activities. After a big "Bombyashke", which we carried out near Bialystok, in the village of Karakul, we came to the 56th "dzhelyanke" in Ozover forest, bringing comrades from all groups to us to distribute the things they needed. After being on the road all night, we rested during the day under the cold autumn sun, which already made the body tremble when lying on the ground. The groups camped scattered in the woods, some talking, some teaching the newly arrived comrades how to handle a rifle, which unfortunately many did not know until the last minute. Quite a few comrades stood at their posts, everything was as normal as every day.

While we are sitting comfortably, we hear a shot, very close. We are not surprised, but after a minute a fierce shooting of "pulemyotn" and [other] automatic weapons begins. Our commander orders us to get up and says that this is certainly a raid. The Germans go through the forest shooting to hear [a reaction in the form of] a shot from us so they know where we are. He orders us to position ourselves at certain points between the trees, and at the moment when he has not even given the second order, we already hear close shouts of the Germans. There are ten men next to us. We see them face to face, coarse, flattened visages, swinish abominations. We open a fierce gunfight, the battle lasts half a day, a mixture of hellish noise and a whistling of bullets in the dense silence of the forest. I am surrounded by Germans! Comrade Khilek with the second "pulemyot" runs to me and helps me to get away from them, opening a gunfight behind my back. At that moment I take a step back

Page 95

and stand side by side with him. A young tree falls from a bullet and crashes down on me. I fall and the next bullet hits my comrade Khilek! I turn my head to him; my comrade Khilek immediately turns pale, falls down, the "pulemyot" lies on him, with the barrel stretched upwards. He holds it tightly with his hands. I look around. No one there. The bullets hit the trees, and leaves fly through the air. I retreat, not knowing which direction is better, but I go back. After 50 meters I meet a comrade who has also shot all his bullets and is retreating. Together we go back to the rear and after some time we sit down, listening to what continues to happen.

I tell him about the death of the comrade at the pulemyot, and he tells me about the death of our commander, which he witnessed. We decide to lie down until the fighting calms down and then take stock. We hear a few more shots and then the hammering of bayonets. They have already reached our kitchen where the cookware is! When it has become dark, we hear the sound of vehicles, apparently the Germans are already leaving. We make our way to the appointed place where we usually meet to see who is missing and who is coming back.

Deep in the darkness of the night we find some of our comrades who join us at the meeting point. Twenty men gather there, ten missing. We decide to go back to the place immediately at dawn to find out what is going on with the 10 men. When we get to the place where our post was, we see him lying face down with his shirt covered with blood - dead! Lying on his post, he immediately shot when he saw the Germans to let us know, as it was agreed. The Germans immediately responded by firing fiercely in his direction, hitting him instantly. The other, who was standing with him and ran to inform us,

Page 96

was slightly wounded in his hand, one finger was shot off. We found him a few days later at a meeting place he knew and where he was waiting for us. When we go deeper [into the forest], we hear a voice. We run there and find a female comrade with a hand shot off, just hanging on by a piece of flesh. Our comrade Rivke Shinder got dumdum bullets and lay there until we found her, after high blood loss. We take her and slowly lead her away to another place. Of the remaining comrades we know nothing yet. After two days we find our comrade Simkhe Love [Lowe], wounded on his leg by a bullet, he was laying there the whole time. He had moved a bit away from the place, so we had a hard time finding him. Six comrades fell, along with our commander, three are wounded and one, Farber, who came to us not long ago from fighting in the ghetto, not knowing of our life there and of the meeting places in the forest, is completely missing. We have no clue as to where he went and whether we should count him among the dead or the living; nor do we know whether the Germans still found him alive.

From the surrounding peasants we learn that among the Germans there are three dead and one wounded, and the biggest enemy, the then spy Karpovitsh, who led the Germans to us, also perished in the battle. Learning about his death, the peasants of the whole area breathed more freely and their relationship with us was characterized by trust and sympathy in recognition of this act. They told us a curious story: before he left for the forest with the Germans to lead them to us, he had said goodbye to his family and told them that he was going on a hard job today not knowing if he would be back. He got drunk on it out of a premonition that it might be his last minutes. But his death cost us too much! We lost our commander and 6 comrades as well as all our food, which we did not manage to distribute to the unarmed

Page 97

groups in time; everything fell into the hands of the Germans and we still had less than nothing.

Our wounded we take to another part of the forest, not far from the place [of the raid], for because of the enormous loss of blood they suffered before we found them, they were too weak to be taken any farther away. We bring a doctor to them who was with us. The doctor assesses them, but what can he do without prescriptions. We leave a couple of women with them to take care of them. From the city we bring them bandages, food and prescriptions. We, the armed men, must continue to concentrate on our work with all our strength and decide to go to another forest for the winter, the Budisk [Budzisk] forest, near Sokolke [Sokółka]. Autumn begins with heavy rains and winds. It pours day and night. We are already completely soaked from the rain. We stand in the rain, sleep in the rain, do everything in the rain. It takes hours to start a fire: We take a rough piece of wood, cut a deep hole with the knife to where it is dry, and gradually use up a whole box of matches until, after a long effort, we can make a fire. We have to move the unarmed comrades away from the forest where the wounded are, so that the sick are safer, attention is drawn away from that place and no one comes looking. Meanwhile, we take our food from nature. Morels gathered in the forest and cooked without salt have a taste like death. Anyway, we are so hungry that we eat another spoon, but from all the food we get sick and start to break green bile. We choose another commander, comrade Shepsl Borovik, a brick layer from Bialystok, my comrade, who served with me in the Red Army in 1940. He is like me, also just has the same knowledge, but after all we do need a [commander], and he has a good orientation in the forest, is brave and energetic.

We start our further life from the beginning. The comrades who had moved away to the Knishin [Knyszyn] forest come back in groups; however, not all of them,

Page 98

and they also bring a comrade who got wounded in the foot a week ago. They support him, he is very weakened. They fought many battles there with the Polish partisans and therefore did not get to organize the [escaped] Jews. The Russian groups have not yet returned and we decide to send two of our comrades away to seek contact with them further east. Comrades Marek and Ele Varat bring us help. Winter is approaching and the weather is getting worse. A foul smell is already emanating from the clothes we are wearing, because they are constantly wet due to the continuous rain that is raining down on us.

The Specific Life of a Jewish Partisan

The Jews who came to the forests of Belarus around Baranovitsh [Baranovichi], Minsk, used to meet strong Soviet partisans, well organized with the help of weapons from Moscow. Parachuted down commanders who had previously graduated from partisan schools in Russia, were active in organizing the partisans in the enemy's war zone. They numbered in the thousands, were well armed and could afford to fence in whole kilometers of forest. Even the villages next to the forest were surrounded by partisans, and for months no German foot entered there. The villages paid a levy in the form of food to the partisans. Many partisans camped quietly for months, organizing workshops where they repaired everything needed by those who came or went to fight. At certain times there were raids by the Germans; then, when they mobilized several divisions, there was heavy fighting with many casualties. Sometimes this ended in retreating to other forests, but often they also managed to repel the Germans, whom they taught to "keep their noses out of their forest and have respect for them."

Page 99

In these forests there were no special problems for the Jewish partisans. They fought together with everyone, as in the armies of all countries, distinguishing themselves by special reliability and willingness to fight against the Germans. The fight of our partisan group from Bialystok, however, was quite different, because it was fought by us alone in the small forests around Bialystok, where there could be no "partisan zone" like further east because of the crossings of many main roads and railroad lines. We had to live in small groups and be ready to fight every minute against the Germans, who often ambushed us because they knew our "forces" and understood that 150 or 200 Germans would be enough to stand against us. The Russian groups that were with us in the woods also had better conditions than we did, because they had the contact with us to coordinate the fight against the Germans, but left the problems of general supplies to us. We had the duty to supply all the Jews who came to us from the ghetto with everything they needed. We were not allowed to go away and leave the woods, partly because of concern for the Jews, who had no weapons, and partly because of the contact with the city that our [female] comrades gave us in the form of cooperation with the P.P.R. Mostly it was us who fought the battles with the Germans.

Quite unexpectedly, one day the comrades we sent to the Russian groups with a request for help return; they bring two Russian comrades from the "Kalinin otryad" [Kalinin Military Cohort], Ele Varat and Marek. There is great joy among us, finally we have managed to get help! They tell us about the difficulties until they could reach us, after we had already moved to other places. They came to us with the task to ease our situation and to take some of our comrades to their forests. We designate 5 comrades to take with them

Page 100

and to whom they are to show the way, because before winter comes, only one armed group is to remain here, for which they leave explosive material and give us instructions, which actions we are to carry out: blowing trains off the tracks, and collapsing bridges. They say goodbye to us and leave. We feel a little relieved, they have taken comrades without weapons and now we hope for help. After all, the explosive material to carry out our actions is already there.

The First Snow

In groups we divide further into different forests to get ready for the approaching winter. A group of 20 armed men goes to the Krinker forest to prepare provisions and pits and to give unarmed Jews the opportunity to winter there and to get some winter clothes, because most of them still go barefoot and without clothes. The nights are already frosty and at dawn everything is covered with thin ice. When we go to sleep, we keep waking up because the tips of our toes are already starting to freeze off. We wrap cloths around our feet, but that doesn't help either. So we walk around at night, and during the day the half-extinguished sun warms us. It sends us its rays like a great boon, as if to say: "Here you have a little warmth! Nature is visibly becoming our new enemy, and we have to be careful of her. I stay with 6 comrades in Budisk [Budzisk] forest and wait for the wounded to be brought to us, because we want to create a center at our place, where everyone should gather first. From there we will split up into other forests where groups of us are already positioned. We decide to celebrate on the day of the Russian October Revolution by cooking a better meal. This will be a real holiday that we have been preparing for so long because our fight with the Germans

Page 101

has taken everything away from us and forced us to move to other forests for a while. My comrade Datner and I are the ones who have to cook that day. We go to sleep because we were up all night to get to know the new forest and the surrounding population, to obtain the information necessary for us in relation to the movements of the Germans around us. On one side of the river Supraśl we set up our camp, in the 11th "dzelyanke", very close to the river, to be able to get water. On our side of the river is a small village of 15 houses, they stand at a great distance from each other, people live there quietly and go about their daily work. After being there in the forest for a while, we went into the village to introduce ourselves to the village elder and promise him various things on our part. We make friends with him and assure him that we will not perform "bomyashkes" in the village. In return, they should take care of taxation themselves and provide us with food as much as they can. At the same time they are to pass on to us any new news concerning the Germans. The village was small and mostly inhabited by poor peasants who had very little land at their disposal, so they all took care of us and pledged help. We behaved a little cautiously about their declaration of friendship and checked their attitude toward us for a long time until we were convinced of their complete decency. There was also a sergeant of the Polish army living there, who enjoyed great prestige among the surrounding peasants. He knew about everything that was happening in the whole area. When we gained complete confidence in him, he used to visit us in our "dzhelyanke" and inform us when we were in danger. The village of Dvozhisk [Dworzysk] came in really useful for us in hard times.

It's getting a little warmer, some rays of sunshine sneak up to us through the countless trees and say, "we are already the last messengers of summer for you, take the opportunity and

Page 102

slumber a little!" We do indeed, and after a discussion in which two opinions emerge, namely that the village can be fully trusted - or that we should be rather cautious, we set two guards and go to sleep. Our feet we stretch to the ashes of the fire, maybe they will not freeze, so we can take a nap.

Either I was asleep, or I was lying there restlessly as usual, opening my eyes from time to time and seeing that everyone else continued to lie there tightly covered, in any case I heard a comrade calling for me: "Kot, stavay! (Kot, get up!)". I pick myself up and it becomes dark before my eyes, that is, I mean actually, it becomes light! I am lying there completely covered with snow and all the comrades next to me are white from snow that fell on us while we were sleeping. We did not notice anything. It got maybe a little wet while lying, but who makes a big fuss about it, is it perhaps a rarity that it is wet? Now we are even more separated from everything. We can't take a step outside, everything is cut off from us at once, there is still so much work for us to do, and then there is this snow! We can't even fetch water or cook anything. What bad luck, we collect snow together with mud from the earth, try to melt this on the fire so that we have water; and from the leaves and the earth together with the snow that fell, we cook our holiday lunch in honor of the October Revolution. One can well imagine the taste of this lunch, because the water was black and stank. But the other comrades said that I had cooked excellently, one should send such a lunch to an exhibition.... No way to clarify the water. We console ourselves that the first snow will melt and then we can organize. Meanwhile, we agree not to sit idly but to build a "zemlyankle", that is, a cottage for the winter, because in winter we can no longer live on the earth as in summer. We decide to dig a pit from three to 4 square meters. The height should be 180 cm. We cut young trees and

Page 103

position them around the walls and as a roof so that no sand is poured in. [We construct] an opening to go out, a special place by the door for the weapons and a small stove made of clay; in the middle comes a cot made of young trees. When you lie down on it, the knots of branches sting you all over your body. While we were building the mud hut, the snow thawed a little. Immediately we decided to take advantage of the weather as soon as possible and bring the wounded comrades from the other woods to us, as well as to arrange the other groups because of the early onset of winter. But what an astonishment to learn that the five we sent out with the Russian comrades, as well as our comrades who had come to accompany them, return only halfway. They met Germans, had a fight with them and could not continue the way. The snow had betrayed their tracks and they had to come back and stay with us for the time being. From this military cohort they returned to us alone by another route; they could not take along any unarmed comrades. So we continue to stay with more comrades; with the wounded we are a group of 20 men in our "dzhelyanke". The snow continues to fall and we remain sitting in place wondering what happened to the rest of our comrades who moved to the Krinker forest to ease our situation.

The Further Life

Every day new snow falls, no trace that it was once summer. The birds have already left us, even those who already knew us and always came at noon, only to grab a piece of meat and flee from the kitchen when the cook just turned to the side as if he did not see it.

At night we cook food. Every day the portions are getting smaller,

Page 104

because the snow is getting higher every day. We already eat nothing solid and no more salt, just a little water with barley that we grind every day from rye. We have to look for a single barley with ten eyeglasses to find it in the so-called "soup". All day long we sit around, huddled together because of the frost, and at night, when we start cooking the food, we warm ourselves on the wood, of which we have enough. Every night we cut down a pine tree and burn it. Our eyes burn from the smoke that rises from our stove, and often it is so smoky that we can't see each other even though we are all so close together. When one of us wants to turn around, he has to tell the other, "Khayim, move back a little, I want to turn around...".

Five comrades are busy cooking. Two chop wood all night, one watches, and two scrape snow into buckets so we have water. Those who have no place [on the cot] sleep during the day, while the others go on watch or walk from one wall to another to warm their feet.

As for laundry, we've agreed that it's one person's turn every three weeks. Every morning everyone shakes out dozens of lice. As for the question of lice, we have already become regular philosophers, dividing them into different groups. However, we wondered what they actually live on, when we ourselves are starving. All comrades begin to develop ulcers, and no sooner has one healed than the next soon follows in the same place. We don't have any medication, our doctor talks about "hygiene", but we sleep one next to the other, no matter whether healthy or sick, and so we are already laughing at his theories. Finally, our wounded heal completely without medicines and diets. The best cure would have been if they had food. We have no news from anyone. The Russian groups are not coming back either; even if they wanted to come, it would not be possible because of the snow. Little by little we run out of everything. One cigarette must be enough for 20 men. Everyone takes a drag, a smack with the lips, and passes the cigarette on; and already there are no cigarettes left either. We collect oak leaves, dry them from

Page 105

the snow and smoke them rolled up in a newspaper. During the day we do not consume a single match to light a cigarette, because we have few matches left to make fire. Days and weeks go by like this. The snow pours more every day.

New Year 1944

Heavy snowstorm. Snow and wind swirl around, the fire goes out and all the smoke is on us. For three hours already we've been trying to get some water boiling, and it hasn't even warmed up yet. The comrades ask one after another: "What about the food? It's New Year's Day. The cook promised a holiday meal!" "There is cleaner water! New snow has fallen!", someone jokes, and a second remarks: "How long has it been since I drank clean water? Certainly quite a few months before the last visit to the village, and there also only from a well; from a tap we have not drunk for almost a year!"

While we are sitting there talking about various things, suddenly five comrades, completely covered with snow, come in to us from a second site seven kilometers away, where 15 comrades have set up with the commander, and inform us that the commander and they have decided to take advantage of the heavy snowstorm that will cover the human footprints. One could certainly go to our familiar village to get food and take advantage of the New Year's Eve when the Germans get drunk and are not careful in the forest. A discussion starts whether we should leave, because the heavy snowfall could stop within minutes, and then everything would be lost. What should we do? Each one says his opinion, but the hunger greatly influences the opinions of the comrades and we decide to go to the village of Dvozhisk [Dworzysk], which is 7 kilometers away from us. The weapons are quickly cleaned and ten of our comrades leave. Heaven and earth intermingle, the wet snow slaps

Page 106

your face and it takes your breath away. The snow reaches to the belt, everything around us is white, you can recognize absolutely nothing. Near the village we can already see light in the huts, and when we imagine how warm and cozy it is now in the rooms, it warms our hearts.

We set up a few posts and go to the village. This time the dogs don't bark as usual, because in such weather it would be a sin even to drive dogs out. We go to the house of the village elder. Around his table, as usual, the peasants are sitting drinking liquor and talking politics. When we come in, they are happy and immediately ask how we can stand it in this weather. But we don't want to stay long and leave the village as soon as possible, not risking the stop of the snowstorm. We inquire about the frequent shootings we hear in the forest. We are told that the Germans go outside to find human tracks in the snow and recently encountered a Russian group. It was attacked and there were many casualties on both sides. They [in the village] thought that something had happened to us too and were happy to see us back in one piece. He determines which houses we may go to get food and we leave his house. The village is noisy with singing and shouting lingering from the houses, to welcome the new year. In every house we enter, it is bright and cheerful, everyone sits there wishing that the war had never been and so many people had to bleed for it. However, the village only dimly feels all the tragedy of the world. The arrival of us, snowed in and frozen as we are, startles them a bit and interrupts their quiet gathering. Our weapons and looks penetrate them and create consternation, they feel a little guilt or a sense that they are just sitting and having a good time, right in the center of the events.

The cold that penetrates us through the open door freezes their faces and there is an expression of guilt in them for sitting there and not going to defend themselves. They bring us the news that the Red Army entered and took already the first town of the former Poland, Sarne [Sarny], and that we will soon be liberated. We do not want to leave the room. The warmth envelops us and reminds us of normal life. But there is no time to think; we open the sacks, pour in what is meant for us and leave the village. When we are already several kilometers away from the village, suddenly the snowstorm stops and we stop abruptly and exchange glances with each other. Our footsteps from the village to the forest are visible like a main road, we must not take one more step! We already know, each for himself, that tomorrow the dogs will be with us—the Germans; that's for sure. We feel even heavier, what to do now? How can we walk when every footstep indicates where we are? Instinctively, everyone reaches for his weapon and checks his rifle. There is silence— several minutes in the dark whiteness of the forest—until someone calls out: "We all go to one of our positions so that when they come, they will only go there and other locations of our group will not be betrayed as well. We send three comrades to bring food to another group and tell them to be ready to fight, everyone else goes to one position!" Without discussion we carry the food and every step in the forest on the white snow threatens a piece of life and makes our looks colder and more piercing. I am one of the three men who go to the second location, but we do not have to wait long and as soon as it becomes daylight, we hear heavy shooting and counter-shooting already in the forest. We know immediately that our group is already there fighting with the Germans. The other comrades, who had come after the meal together with the commander, had immediately packed up and set up a post to watch the path that led through the whole forest to their "dzhelyanke". He was instructed not to shoot at the Germans from his post, but only to report when he saw them coming. As soon as he stood, he saw them following the steps to the [partisan] place, but he could not count them. The commander immediately orders to divide into two groups; one in

one direction, and the second in the other. Seven men go with the commander, Shepsl Borovik; and the remaining 15 comrades, together with a comrade from the city, Malke Vyezhebitski, [Wiersbitzky?], who had joined us in the winter, in a second direction. The Germans went hunting on the trail of the smaller group with the commander, pursuing them for a whole day.

Fighting until late evening, they [the partisans] lost 6 comrades and the commander. One of them managed to save himself. Among the Germans there were two dead. One comrade spent two days in the forest and knew that he was not allowed to go to any group because every step he took was visible and could kill the whole group he was going to. But the hunger and the cold forced him to go to a forester who lived in the forest and ask for food. The latter gave him some, but sent his wife out the back door to report it to the Germans. The Germans arrived, surrounded the house with weapons, arrested [the comrade] and took him alive to Supraśl to their staff, tortured and beat him to make him betray the places where the partisans were. However, he did not betray them. They then dressed him in German clothes, gave him the finest of food and drink, promising him that they would let him live if he told them whether he had been in the village and whether the village elder had given them food. They brought in the village elder and arranged for a lineup. He [the comrade], however, kept a combative attitude and announced that he absolutely did not know him and was seeing him for the first time. Thereupon the German said to the village elder: "The Jew saved you and the whole village, because I know for a fact that you gave him food!"

When they realized that they could not get anything out of him, they tried a last resort. They led him into the forest to show where [the partisans] lived. However, he led them to other places, far away from the right one, and they shot him. That's how heroically our comrades fought, each one of them, in whatever situation they

Page 109

were, always showed heroism. The village appreciated this and continued to support us constantly and with even more confidence.

The remaining groups stayed in the forest until the snow thawed a little and then joined a group that lived in the Supraśl Forest, however, everyone had to live standing up there because there was nothing to lie down on. Only the little bit of food that was frozen from being carried around for so long saved them. In winter, one could not look for a new site and had to continue living under these conditions. The snow that fell every day isolated us. After New Year's Day, we received no news from any of the surrounding groups spread out in the woods about their situation. However, every morning we heard new gunfire from the Germans in the surrounding area, who went around looking for our whereabouts. The reason was that in the village where we were at New Year's Day, a man who was the son of the miller from Myendzhizhetsh [Międzyrzecze], had just visited a girl there. He revealed to the Germans that we had been in the village, which voluntarily paid us taxes in the form of food. (We learned about this only later).

The food we brought from the village did not last long; we did not even talk about going out again to get more. The snow does not thaw and every day it is the same program: early in the morning the roosters would crow from the village (because of the silence of the forest it can be heard very far), and in the noon hours there are shootings. Our constant hunger, which does not want to disappear, but becomes stronger and stronger, forces us to think about how to go on. We have to go out! After all, there are often snowstorms! But we don't want to say it out loud, too many sacrifices our walk has cost us at that time. We elect comrade (Kole) Nyome Kirzhner as commander, in place of our deceased commander Shepsl Borovnik. Anyway, without us changing anything [in the planning], nobody

Page 110

wants to take responsibility for the instruction [to go outside]. We discuss everything, everyone has their say. As always, it's evening and we have to heat up and cook smaller and smaller portions that you don't even want to look at after sharing; in the end it's just sometimes a little less water and sometimes a little more, it doesn't matter. After the meal, we really get an appetite. It would be better not to eat. That's why we've already gotten out of the habit of waiting for dinner to cook. We comrades lie there and get ulcers on our bodies. One gets well, three others get sick. The doctor doesn't even look at us anymore, what should he look at if we have no medicine. We try to find a way out, and after a week of discussion we decide that four comrades should go out and cover their footprints with snow behind them. The four comrades are to go to a village, take a horse there, which will be killed later to provide us with food, but also to make people think we are going far away. Of necessity, most of the comrades agree, and those who are destined go. They return immediately, however, and report that the small bridge across the river that we used to cross has broken apart, apparently caused by the ice. We cannot cross it.

So yet another problem, now what? We continue to think and discuss. Comrade Motl Tshremoshne, a carpenter, suggests we build a raft and swim across. We saw off trees and tie them together with rags of torn clothes. We carry them to the river and twist two ropes, one pulling from one side of the river, the second from the other. So we put our comrades across to the other side. I, with the machine gun, am to go last. The raft is covered with ice; it is such a strong frost that every little bit of water that splashes onto the raft immediately freezes into ice. As soon as I step on the raft, I slip and, together with the machine gun, fall into the river. They pull me out, completely frozen. I first put the machine gun on the raft to get it across alone, and after that it is easier for me to get across to the other side. Two comrades

Page 111

leave me the task of hiding the raft well to come back on it. We now have to walk 15 kilometers to get to the designated place. The snow is up to our necks in some places, steam rises from everyone's clothes, but we all feel such a great responsibility to complete the task that we force ourselves with the last of our strength to move forward.

Late at night we reach the village. Darkness around us, single, scattered and snow-covered huts, only the chimneys look out. We knock, a peasant in underpants comes out, opens and is immediately frightened: "In this weather, with weapons, from where?" We don't let him think long, ask him for the key to the barn and a lamp. He goes out with us, we take his horse and tell him that he will get it back tomorrow, as always. We lead the horse halfway into the woods, kill it and divide it up for the sacks of our comrades. We leave a remnant. At dawn we return to our location. The comrades are already waiting impatiently, and when they learn that everything went exactly as we had decided beforehand, they are very pleased. Soaked as we came, we stay the whole day, and none of us who left coughed even once! One of them calls out, [referring to me]: Now, after I fell with all my things into the river and froze to a piece of ice, then walked such a long distance, marched back and everything was in the best order afterwards, he understands why the wild animals in the forest do not need a doctor. Everyone is happy, we already have food for three weeks, pure horse meat! So the weeks drag on and the winter has us firmly in its grip, always in the worst conditions. Full of energy to fight, we unfortunately do not have the opportunity to use our weapons; but our courage and devotion to each other increase greatly. The conversations we have among ourselves fill us with satisfaction; there is no comparison with the leadership of the ghetto, which was the opposite of our attitude! They are the same Jews, from the same city, and yet they are different in every way.

Page 112

The Day of the Red Army
(February 23, 1944)

The Red Army is on all fronts and getting closer and closer to us. Other comrades already hear certain explosions and try to convince us that they are Soviet artillery shells. Every single one comes running out from above and asks the guard if he doesn't hear anything. The hope arises to be able to go out to "pay the German" a little for the hard winter and our fallen comrades and to show him that we are still there! "He" is not rid of our group yet, as he thinks. All of our conversations revolve around liberation but we can't go out and blow something up in the summer like we used to. We have to be content with cooking something completely different than usual to create a festive spirit. During the meal, comrades tune in with stories about the Red Army, its founding and its combat tasks. We have designated a comrade especially for this day [February 23] to prepare the meal. The meat we ate from for three weeks has already been used up, but the horse's "kishke" [intestine] is still there, and our "comrade cook" has agreed to prepare a proper "kishke and cholent" as it used to be, in good times. We explain to our Russian comrade who is with us how Jewish "kishke and cholent" tastes, and that it is so delicious that the letter carrier who used to deliver our letters came especially to eat with us when there was "cholent and kishke".

For the holiday, people are busy crafting. The kishke is filled with some potatoes we found. That day we hear a very close shooting, more violent than usual, but we already do not even pay attention to it. At 12 noon, by our reckoning anyway, we sit down to celebrate the feast in our primitive way, due to the living conditions. It is comrade Khayim's turn to keep watch. It doesn't suit him at all that he has to go out and keep watch for an hour at such an important time when everyone

Page 113

is preparing, but it's no use and off he goes.

The "kishke" is soot-blackened, outside and inside, plus too much has been stuffed into it, so it could barely cook through. We all eat, smacking our lips and looking at our Russian comrade to see how he likes it. We eat and reminisce about that time; but he must be wondering what kind of food it is, and if it was worth waiting so long for it and listening to all the explanations about it! The comrades begin to talk, but in the middle of it we hear our comrade Khayim Khalef shouting, "Stoy" [Stop!]. We don't grasp the situation yet, but suddenly there is a heavy firing from an automatic weapon; we grab our weapons and run out, partly barefoot, partly wearing a shoe, and see our comrade lying on the ground and a person in civilian clothes fleeing with a machine gun. We run to our comrade Khayim and he tells us that the unknown man was running towards him, he wanted to stop him but the other one started shooting, whereupon [Khayim] immediately fell down. We decide to leave the place because we don't know who the unknown person is and what the all-day shooting is about. There is snow all around us, every step reveals where we are, but we choose to spend a whole day and night walking around in the forest on different paths to cover our tracks. Late in the evening the shooting ends and we decide, to go back to the site from which our group was expelled on New Year's Day, to rest. We do not dare to go to other groups, because that could also mean having to stay in the snow for months. We approach the site and everyone instinctively feels fear to go in there, where it is dark and reminds of each of the comrades who were with us in so many battles, and went through the hardest time until they perished on New Year's Day. For the time being, however, we must remain here in the same place where our best comrades lost their lives, but who, in view of their fighting and human attitude, will be a pioneering example for others in the future, because their perseverance

Page 114

and their struggle against injustice has not been in vain. The struggle will be carried on by the remaining comrades in memory of those who perished.

We reinforce the posts, because comrade Datner left in another direction during the shooting at us and is now missing; we don't know what happened to him. So we lie in the new site for three days, completely without food, because we left in a hurry and couldn't take anything with us; and here everything is smashed by the Germans who were there. The snow is starting to thaw a little, and [the moisture] is trickling in through the earth to us. Our only worry is, what happened to our comrade Datner? Once, while standing guard, I see a person coming toward us from a distance, but I can't see him clearly because of the trees. I put out a report to everyone and [comrades] come out and position themselves in the snow. How stunned are we when a comrade observing the person exclaims: "There goes Datner!" We are all trembling with surprise; he can hardly drag himself to us, with his sack on his back and his rifle in his hand. I am the first to run to meet him and cover him with kisses, followed by all the others. With tears in our eyes we welcome each other. Our joy at that moment was indescribable!

We learn from Comrade Datner that he was in the village of Dvozhisk [Dworzysk] during the three days and hid with the village elder. The Germans had a fight that day with a Russian group 5 kilometers from us. There were many dead on both sides, and the person who ran to us was a Russian partisan of that group, whom the Germans shot at and whose tracks they followed. He did not know that we, in our place, [were on his side] and when he heard the exclamation of our comrade "Stoy!" he thought that we were Germans who continued to pursue him. Therefore, he immediately fired and retreated. For us this was a very big blow. We were not allowed to return to the other place because when [Datner] was in the village,

Page 115

he learned that the Germans were bringing reinforcements and were setting about checking the forest for human footprints that had been carried all over the forest after the fighting. So, in the meantime, we have to stay here until the snow, which gives us no possibility of operations, thaws. The next few days pass us by with difficulty, but they are already the last! The month of March has arrived and the sun is already beginning to warm us a bit during the day. Surely the snow in the city has already completely thawed away; but here we live with appropriate hope. The few potatoes that Datner brought from the village is for the time being the only food for 15 men. We build a small stove of wood, which constantly goes out, and we have to build a new one every few days. In April, all our food supplies are already used up and we decide to go out.

Our first walk is to our former hiding place, which we had left; we want to see what has become of it, and besides, comrade Datner left a loaf of bread there 6 weeks ago. We calculate that this will make 120 grams of bread for each comrade, and that would be a great joy! We choose 6 comrades to go ahead and, if possible, go to the village to find out what is going on in the area. I am one of the 6 comrades; we set our footsteps only where grass can be seen. When we get to our old mud hut, 7 kilometers from our new location, we find that the bread has since been eaten by a mouse. Only the old, upper crust remains. Instead of 120 grams, there are now only 20 grams left for everyone. Everyone takes their piece of bread and chews each bite well before swallowing it. The pleasure and taste of that piece of bread, which was hard as stone, frozen and nibbled by a mouse, and smaller than a "kezais" [the smallest portion of food counted as food in the Talmud], I will remember all my life. Even now, when I already have the opportunity to eat the best food, yet I have never had so much pleasure from a meal as I did then from that little bit of

Page 116

bread. Afterwards we go to the village and learn that the front is already very close to us. We decide to return and advise our comrades that we should prepare to go out, to begin to revive with the Spring that will bring us the possibility to move freely, to re-establish contacts with all those who are in the forest and to make the Germans pay for our sufferings and fallen comrades.

We Are Back!

The new Spring presents itself to us as a savior from the psychological and physical sufferings of the whole winter, which have so strongly affected our limbs. With each of us who has gone through it, the feeling of successive sufferings remains, and each of my comrades who was with me will remember it; he, when he tells of it, will constantly endure the long influence of a great pain, while he cannot make the listener sympathize with it all. However, there is no force that can change the course of nature: The sun destroys all the snow and wipes it off the surface, creating a path for us to the new life that begins with us crawling out of our mud huts onto the open earth and spreading out over all parts of the forest, shouting our slogan: "We are back!"

The front is already very close to us; the Germans are focusing all forces in various ways to find us. They make Ukrainians and Belorussians put on civilian clothes, send them into the forest as partisans to get to us and uncover our [hiding places]. We engage in many battles with them, which cost us and them victims. All this, unfortunately, prevents for a long time our meeting with the Russian groups, which are already on the way to look for us and bring help. The large-scale

Page 117

movements of us back in the forest led to a meeting with the old Russian partisan groups that had begun to move toward our forest area. When we went to the village at night to get various information about the area, we also met a group of Russian partisans. But due to the experience in previous places, where we met Ukrainians, whom we had to face to fight, now we also started a fight

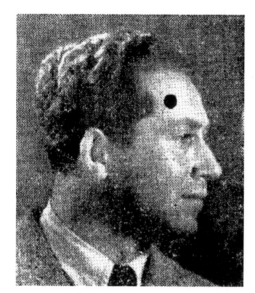

With my comrade in battle, Khalif

not knowing who they really were, and retreated without casualties. The moment of meeting came later, in places that were more familiar to us and about which the peasants had told us that they had seen Russian partisans there. Once, walking in the darkness of a rainy spring night, a group that did not oppose us to fight stopped us. We sent comrades to them to see who they were, and how great was our joy,

Page 118

when a comrade recognized the former Russian comrades who had been with us that summer and had assured us then that they would return. They came with many new partisans from organized military cohorts who had the task of going into our forests and making further preparations for the Red Army. In their forests they left only small groups and moved almost all to our area.

Many of the comrades we asked about died during the battle and many of our comrades, who were known to the others and with whom they did various jobs, also fell in the meantime. We welcome them because it is decided that with us will be the meeting place for all who will arrive. They will also bring their "Kombrig" (brigade commander) who will unite us all into a military cohort.

The final day of the meeting we had been waiting for so long was approaching. Every day new Russian partisans come to us from their military cohort, and all of us are now waiting for the staff with the "kombrig", which will finally officially accept us into the Soviet partisan federation, according to the laws of the partisan army. Until the arrival of the staff, all Russian groups that are coming in are staying with us. We already feel very strong. Many machine guns and automatic weapons have been brought by the Russian comrades. It already doesn't matter whether you are in the forest by day or by night;

meanwhile we go when we want and where we have to, right under the nose of the Germans. The forest is turned into a front with all the main communications. We already have radios transmitting directly from Moscow various information and instructions on which sections to be active. We hurry to gather all our comrades from the different forests and bring them to us with the news that finally the moment they have long waited for has arrived: Our trusted old comrades came back, with whom we will have the opportunity

Page 119

to make the necessary arrangements to liberate our city and area. All our groups have been severely affected by the winter with its difficult, superhuman conditions. One group lost 90%, the other two suffered extremely from the lack of provisions but managed to avoid human casualties. The comrades from Bialystok worked continuously during the winter after they lost contact with us; and when the snow melted, they brought to us quite a few comrades who helped [others] to escape from the Bialystok prison or assisted those who were persevering still in the city in various ways. Berl Shatsman and others have arrived. We gather everything and all [comrades] together, all our material and strength, to present ourselves to the staff that will come to us.

Our Official Connection to the Partisan Family

We have all gathered now and are waiting for the staff to finally be connected, after waiting for so long! [At last] many well-armed partisans arrive at our place together with the "Kombrig", Voitshekhovski [Woyczechowski]. He is a tall man in good physical condition, with a very intelligent face and many medals for leading the partisan struggle. During the war he was specially flown from Moscow and parachuted for the tasks in the woods. There are also women with German rifles, which they captured in the battles, on their way to our forests. The general outward appearance of the "kombrig" evokes a great awe in us, more than anyone else who has come with the staff. We all sit down and tell about all our struggle until the time we met. Our contact with the city will now be used

Page 120

by the staff on more important sections. We sit there for a whole day and report on the entire course of the fighting and conditions in the forests. We also tell about our connections with the individual farmers of the surrounding villages.

The staff recognizes all our work, perseverance and persistence under these conditions and with so few weapons. At the same time, he announces that he will give us the same credit for all the time we were alone as if we had belonged to the brigade earlier. He asks us to decide whether we want to continue to exist as an independent Jewish group with our commander or whether we no longer want to be detached. But then we would be distributed among all the divisions of the brigade, and in each military cohort there would be a part of us. We decide to be sent to all military cohorts and to take equal part in all the tasks that are imposed on us. The "kombrig" accepts our decision. We are divided among the whole brigade. One part goes to the "Matrosov" detachment with the name " Geroy Sovetskovo Soyuza Matrosov" [Matrosov, Hero of the Soviet Union], a small part is taken over to the staff to work there, and the third part, in which I was, goes to another militia cohort with the name "26 Yor Oktyober Revolutsye." [26 Years of October Revolution]. One detachment with the name of its commander, Andryev, the "Andreyevtsn", consists of the dropped paratroopers, and the fourth detachment consists of Belarusians of the same area. We say goodbye to the comrades who were with us for so long; and actually, they stay together even now, although each division goes in a different direction. We scatter over the entire length of all forests from Volkovisk to Knishin [Knyszyn]. We are dispersed to all places there and meet only from time to time when we pass through a forest for certain works and sabotage actions. Then we used to discuss with the comrades, each of whom can tell something about blown up trains, fights with Germans on the main roads and night raids on the vehicles they are driving. Documents and pictures are shown,

Page 121

which were taken from the dead Germans, including their weapons. We also get to see Ukrainians captured in battles; Germans are less likely to be captured alive.

Our life becomes more interesting and active every day. A small part of comrades is very exhausted from the winter and sit in the mud huts until they come to themselves again.

My group moves to another site. I, too, have to rest for a few days and cannot do anything because of my weakness. However, I am quickly regaining my strength and after that I am again doing my due part; for now, in such an interesting time we are facing, is no time to be ill. In each section, we, the newcomers, take an oath, as required by military law. My commander Filipov, also a paratrooper who went through partisan training and is a lieutenant, calls for me: "Have you rested enough, have you recovered? We are to go to the Krinker Forest now, and you have been appointed to do so, too!" I still feel weak, but I would be ashamed to say that I cannot yet, and answer: "Healthy or sick, it doesn't matter. I just have to go along!" I have waited so long for this time, and now I am supposed to be sick?! I am angry with myself. In the evening we set out for several weeks, 8 men with the commander Filipov, a nurse (a Russian woman who came with the commander). Armed with automatic weapons, a machine gun and rifles, we go through forests where we find our groups widely scattered, and in each of the sites, we hide. Along the way, we introduce our commander to all our trusted farmers who have provided us with connections and news. Our commander now gives them new tasks to perform. When we reach the railroad junction Volkovisk, we meet one of our groups and stay there for a day. It is determined that a train should be blown off the tracks, in the middle of the day and not at night as usual. The commander of the other group puts on the uniform of a German railroad official and goes out on the tracks

Page 122

pretending to repair something. Lying in the forest, we prepare the explosive material and wait for the train to come. We can already hear the sound of the wheels; our excitement is growing by the minute. Soon the German sons of bitches will feel the new summer coming upon them. A sign from the commander. We run to bring the material there and then retreat. When we have already run 30 meters from the spot, we fall down by the shock wave of the violent explosion and hear screams of people, later also shots, from the same direction. We get up and go further into the forest. Later we learn from the surrounding farmers that the action was very successful: German soldiers were on their way to the front by train and had to "pay" there! Many dead and wounded, over 30 of these dogs. The peasants are satisfied, and when we visit a village, they ask incessantly when the Red Army will finally come, which is so close. It takes them too long and they have no more patience.

We continue to the Krinker Forest on "trails and paths" over marshes that have never been trodden by a human foot, not even that of God. Mud up to over the knee, so that one thinks never again to be able to crawl out. We are led by a Belorussian whom we met in the forest; he fled from Germany, where he was deported to work. At his home, in Mikhalove [Michałowo], he hid a rifle before the war, which he now wants to dig out. At night we position ourselves near his village and keep watch in the surrounding area. He goes with two men to his family to dig out the rifle. The night is starry and bright. We wait for him. Suddenly, from a distance, we see a group of people moving in our direction. We let them come closer to us and then shout: "Stoy! Kto idyot? (Stop! Who goes there?)" "Russians," they shout and go on. This answer is worth nothing, because they would have to answer "Partizani!" and stop. We shout for them to stop, if not, we shoot. They stop. We give instructions that one

Page 123

person from them and one from us should walk forward to face each other. Comrades of ours and of theirs step forward, and when they meet, they embrace and squeeze hands. We now know that they are partisans, and we all walk toward them. We learn that they are a group of Russian prisoners who escaped from Germany. They had been in Warsaw all this time, on the other side of the Bug River, but they had to leave that area and move further east because the Polish partisans were chasing them. The last battle they fought with these "Polyakn" forced them to leave those forests. The falsehood of the Polish partisans went so far that they first made an agreement with [the Russian partisans] not to attack each other, after which they were even invited to their camp for talks, to continue the fight together. But the "Polyakn" took advantage of the visits to the camp of the Soviet partisans; at first they spied on the forces of the group, and on their third visit, when precautions had already ceased to be taken in the camp and everyone was allowed to move about freely, two "Polyakn" at a time sat down next to a Russian or a Jew. This was their strategy, and when the Russians were completely guileless, sitting together and talking like the times before, suddenly the Polish commander gave a signal, and each "Polyak" shot at the Russian partisans sitting next to them. The battle was terrible; the sudden attack brought great losses to the Russians. More than half of them perished, the rest gathered and decided to move further east.

They divided into two groups, both moving in the same direction, but only one arrived at our place, without knowing what became of the second. We also learn that together with them came a Jew who remained alive after the fight with the "Polyakn". Out of 20 Jews, he was the only one left. We seek him out and learn from him that after the fighting in the Warsaw Ghetto, he fled with those Jews who had now perished in the fighting. He remained all alone,

Page 124

He is young, only 17 years old and speaks a poor Yiddish. He is surprised by the meeting with the Red Army and, at the same time, with us.

The way in which the "Polyakn" fought for liberation was best shown to us by the facts they [the Russians] handed over to us. During the day the "Polyakn" lived as free citizens in the villages, and at night they went armed into the forests to search for and murder Russians and Jews. This was their struggle, which helped the Germans more than it harmed them. We take the group with us and decide to turn back after we meet a group of Białowieża partisans in the Krinker Forest, who tell us that this is their forest and we are not allowed to stay there for long. At first, they also wanted to take over the Russian group, because they thought it belonged to them, since we had found it in their forest. But we agreed: they should belong where they themselves wanted to go. We knew that in order to be safer they would have to go further east, and when we told them that we too would go back east to our forests, the result was that 90 percent went with us and only some who had found a few acquaintances in the other partisan group stayed with them. We now returned with 20 more comrades with machine guns and rifles. At night, when we passed the place where the railroad was blown up, we heard how they were working there to put the rails back up. After that, we decided that a large group should go to a village during the day to pick up the milk that the village had already prepared for the Germans. This made such an impression on the village that the children ran into the houses with joy, exclaiming, "The Red Army has come!"

When we get back to our woods, we learn that in the meantime large searches by Germans and Ukrainians have taken place in our camps. At the agreed point we meet our

Page 125

elder who leads us away. We learn of a new stand for which we all have to go back into the Knyszyn woods. On this walk we shell a vehicle with Germans in it. We take one prisoner alive, a Russian in German clothes, and of course "he is quite innocent". He comes from Voronyezh [Voronezh], fighting all the time on the side of the Germans. He gets his "earnings" from us. Military cohort "Matrosov" remains in the woods. The German armies are already partially retreating, and we go to blow up bridges. From the forest we fire on the passing army, which is retreating on the main roads that pass through the forest.

In the Knyszyn Woods

A group of our military cohort has, together with the staff, already left for the Knyszyn woods. I walk with the second and last group. We make it in one night and at dawn we reach the woods of Knyszyn, where we meet our group, which in the meantime, has organized all the Jews they encountered, including several Jewish women. For two years these Jews hid in the forests under the most difficult conditions, where they had to stay from 1942, after all the Jews from the surrounding towns had been deported. They persevered without weapons and bought food from the surrounding farmers. Many of them perished during the time, but a large part persevered and now experienced the longed-for hour.

Page 126

We [finish] organizing all of them, take them to us and, as far as possible, provide them with weapons. We ask them to lead us along the paths they are so bitterly familiar with, and involve them in our activities. However, we soon meet Polish partisans, coming face to face with them. There are a large number of them in the woods, and the surrounding Polish villages are their allies. As we enter the village to gather information about our new location, fire is opened on us! Our comrade, a Russian, is wounded in the hand. We search the village and encounter Polish partisans who, as usual, were shooting at us. We establish a contact with them for cooperation.

We know that they have been fighting us all the time and even shooting at our Russian comrade, but the surrounding area is full of their villages where they have many confidants. We have to join with them, and indeed, a union is coming about. However, they still put the condition that they will not go together with Jews, but the Russians reject it. Meanwhile, it remains that when they go to fight, they go only with the Russians, without us Jews. We, with a part of the Russian partisans, stay in the Knyszyn forest. The staff with a large part of "Polyakn" goes ahead to the "Shilingvukher" swamps around Ostrovyets to continue the fight. For a short time, we are together with the "Polyakn", but we feel very bad among them because at any turn, they show their anti-Semitism, so we go to another part of the forest. All their behavior in the forest [toward us] was provocative.

The Last Weeks and the Day of Liberation

We received a new radio receiver to transmit information to and from Moscow. Our group with its commander, Filipov, and the Jews from the Knyszyn Forest who had joined us, stayed

Page 127

after the staff had left for the Knyszyn forests to continue our work.

The front is already near Bialystok; the fighting for the liberation of our city continues. Every evening and every day Bialystok is heavily bombed. We see Soviet planes flying, dropping missiles that light up the whole forest as bright as day and also give us the opportunity to walk in daylight. The Germans position themselves around our sites with heavy artillery, their constant cannon shots echoing in the forest and making the earth tremble as if it were being cradled. The surrounding peasants lead everything out of the villages, the horses, the cows, the sheep and more precious things, because the retreating Germans grab everything, rob all that is possible and set fire to the villages and towns. The sky keeps turning red from the burnings. We have to dig pits for ourselves where we can lie at times during the frequent shelling of the main roads by the Red Air Fleet [Soviet Air Forces], for they drop very low to fire on the retreating German armies and often hit right into the woods.

Every day we go out of the camp to the edge of the forest to wait for the departing German army and catch them, and then "refresh" ourselves at some Germans for the last weeks. Because the liberation is near, and after the liberation there will be no more such opportunity. Going out to the village of Kopisk, as we always do, from the edge of the forest we see a cart driving, fully loaded with sacks. We hide and wait for it. Not long after, we see 5 young Germans walking right behind the cart, their sleeves rolled up as always when they are at their predatory work. They walk so slowly, as if they don't want to get ahead at all. They stride with their bandit-like equanimity. We let the cart pass, and while [the five] go on, we jump out of the forest, pointing our rifles at them. "Hands up!" we shout to them in German. We take their weapons from them and begin to lead them to us in the forest. One tries

Page 128

to escape, he is shot. A comrade immediately pulls off his good boots. "Hands up!", we shout to them in German. We take their weapons and lead them to us in the forest. One tries to escape, he is shot. To our shot we immediately hear a response from the Germans, who are rushing to help and are standing relatively close around us. There are still a few hundred meters to the forest. Concluding that we can no longer take the Germans because their cavalry is on us, we shoot them and retreat into the woods, where we are at the mercy of a firefight with their cavalry, who chase us all the way to the forest.

It was not a good noon, because their revenge was that they set fire to a house in the village and shot a farmer who applauded joyfully when we seized the Germans. We go on every day and, as always, we surround a main road that leads through the forest. Day and night, very close to the edge of the forest, the German army drives with shouting and roaring. We open fire on them, whereupon their normal ride turns into a commotion and a race. They collide with each other, everyone runs in the direction they can, losing various things. However, we can't hold off for long. After a short shooting from our side, we retreat deeper into the forest and seize 20 armed soldiers in German uniforms. Later, after bringing them to our camp, it turns out that they are Russian citizens from [Andrey Andreyevich] Vlasov's army fighting against the Soviet Union; several Ukrainians, Kazakhs, Uzbeks and others. Each of them claims that they came of their own accord to surrender after fleeing from the Germans and that they did not accompany the [German] army that we just shot at. We assign them a separate place, deciding to detain them and hand them over to the Red Army, which will come in the next few days. Every day they are guarded by a different comrade and it is observed that every day they get rid of more [of their military clothing] and put on civilian clothes to conceal their past.

Bialystok is already liberated, taken by the Red Army. We learn that during the last three days before they retreated,

Page 129

the Germans set fire to all the houses and factories in the city. The front is now in the direction of Knyszyn, only 5 kilometers from us. On all roads and paths the German army is retreating, fighting for every meter of earth. In the last few days, we've been putting up more guard posts outside. We are no longer allowed to cook or make even the smallest fire. Shots and explosions are heard incessantly. We sit there and listen every hour on the radio receiver to the positions that are being taken around us; those that we know, but where we have never been. How indescribable the word "freedom" sounds to us now!

We look at each other and ask ourselves, could it be possible that we are free? No one really can believe that. After all, it means to us that we survived, which creates a sensation that no other participant in the war, except a Jewish one, might feel. The last days it is impossible to leave the forest. One day, it is a little quieter than usual. We sit in separate groups and talk about comrades from the other groups who may already be in Bialystok. Each individual thinks of his home, to which he will quickly return. Suddenly, we hear a noise close to us. A comrade runs to look and soon comes back shouting, "Russian scouts have arrived at our place!" The shouting confuses us all, though; it has all come so suddenly! Especially since we have been used to hearing just silence for the past year and have been wary of a loud word or even a strong cough. Quick as a flash, we all get up and run to look: yes! There is sitting the commander with the scouts in a circle, two young Red Army soldiers, 18 to 20 years old, with automatic weapons in their hands and grenades strapped around them. Their faces are haggard and angular; they are so thin that the belt with the grenades strapped to it barely holds on to them. At once, the whole atmosphere changes. They tell us that from Minsk onwards they, as scouts, have been constantly chasing the Germans. We give them food and, sitting together, we talk about various battles in which they were involved.

Page 130

Their task now is to scout the German forces around Knyszyn. We immediately introduce them to our comrade from Knyszyn; he accompanies them to show them a better and shorter way. After a few days the regular army arrives, which we await with great joy and disbelief. No one can sleep anymore during the day or night. Everyone asks themselves the question: Having arrived at the destination, and now what happens next? For so long we have been waiting for this day! So many Jews have perished, and only we have made it to this extraordinary day. Every Russian who is among us talks about how he will come home to his parents, wife and children, and tell them all he has been through, but to whom can we talk about it? Can we really rejoice in having survived? Have we now achieved freedom? When we come out of the forest and are on the way to the next village, we see the great "rulers", the "victors of the world" lying in the ditches, as objects for dogs and insects, and passers-by spit on them in disgust.

The Red Army soldiers are different from what I remember from 1940. They wear different uniforms, epaulettes and medals for heroism on their chests. But, they are as good-natured interpersonally as before; for four years I did not see them and longed for them. Now convoys full of Red Army soldiers are driving and occupying all the villages in the area. We hand over our prisoners of [Andrey Andreyevich] Vlasov's army to the staff with a document, "captured when they fought against us," and we all go on our way, further below the front, to the position of the staff of partisans, to receive our documents. All the main streets and roads are full of Red Army soldiers moving to the front. But we go back, some in civilian clothes, others in military, each different. The passing army shouts: "Our partisans!" Everyone quarters with a farmer to eat and spend the night. We begin to learn more and more about the great catastrophe that has befallen the Jews, because when the peasants realize that I am Jewish, they tell about it. It becomes more and more burdensome

Page 131

to listen. With the peasant population it causes astonishment when we say that we are Jews. They look at us strangely: How is it possible for a Jew of our region to still be alive?"

Upon Its Own Grave
(Bialystok in August 1944)

After completing all the formalities and handing in the rifle, I turn back to see Bialystok again. I leave with a feeling of "joy" to return to my native city, and at the same time with a cutting pain, asking myself: "What will I find there?" My mind tells me, "nothing at all," but my inner feeling calls out to me, "Maybe yes- a single one?!" I walk 10 kilometers on foot. On the way, farmers are standing in their fields harvesting grain, the scythe cutting as if nothing had happened at all. The villages along the way are partially destroyed, but others still intact. The jars are inverted over the fences, the peasants are in front of their houses having finished their day's work. In one breath I walk ahead, driven by one thought: Bialystok! What does it look like? And who is still there? Arriving in the outskirts I can see the extent of the destruction: Chimneys without houses, all bridges destroyed, the train station burned down; of entire streets only skeletons of masonry are left, and other streets are completely obliterated. You don't even recognize if anything was ever there. Is that really where the people I once knew well lived, people I spent time with? At least memories and a good souvenir will remain forever.... Germans are standing there locked behind a fence. I walk up to them, looking at them with disgust, and ask the Red Army soldier guarding them: "They are still alive?" He answers with a smile: "It is meaningless, they will perish!"

I continue on my street to see the house where I lived and left brother and sister a year ago! I walk in the direction where the ghetto was. My first glance falls

Page 132

on the pavement where, as far as I can remember, the fence had been. 20 meters from the fence the earth is overgrown with grass, so that the stones can hardly be seen. No people have walked here [for a long time], the grass is already firmly grown. Where once the stones had already loosened from so many human footsteps, now grass is growing, and the stones, half-covered, are shouting: "Grass, would you please not cover us? People have to walk here! Jews have

Excavation of the murdered heroes

gone here and built their lives, for generations. We have to tell about it!" All the streets are empty, no people anywhere. All houses destroyed: here walls are missing, there is a house with only one wall, elsewhere the windows and doors are missing. Jewish and other books are lying around on all sides, wherever you just take

Page 133

a look. And if you turn your head: broken furniture, chairs without feet, cupboards without doors, broken beds; it's not worth it to take any of it away. Feathers from quilts are lying there intermingled with photos of people who lived there, photos of Jews with beards and forelocks; Jews without hats, women with "sheytlen" [wigs] or with the most modern hairstyles. The image of a child laughing

The pit, where they have now transferred the remains of the heroes of the ghetto.

and the image of a mother holding the child and rejoicing. A boy on a horse and a fellow in a small "tales" [prayer shawl] with tefillin at his bar mitzvah. These generations full of life and creativity cannot be erased from the earth

Page 134

all at once. Even the earth does not want to swallow this, it lacks the boldness to do so; it leaves everything on its surface, admonishing and crying out: "What did you do? And why?"

My blood freezes as I look at all this, and it upsets me, the tears come. When I get to my street, Bialostotshenski [Białostoczańska],

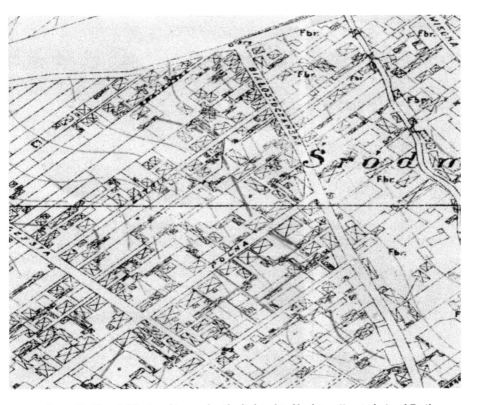

[map: Dr. Tomek Wisniewski, see also the link to his film https://youtu.be/nrc1Gtvjl-c

I walk more slowly; as in the times when they used to tell me that I am about to be shot. The same feeling I have as I approach the house number 19. This is where I lived. Three house numbers before, I can already see that our house no longer exists at all, not even a skeleton has remained that you could look at and run towards, like to your loved ones. Where you could cry, lean in like a little kid just learning to walk and still clinging to the walls. I meet only stones of the foundation and half a chimney. Sand has fallen on it from above and sparse blades of grass have grown. I climb onto the foundations of the house, consider and check where the window has been? Where was the door? Where was my bed? And, where did the picture of my parents hang, which they had taken the week of their happy wedding. We children used to look at how they changed as they got older, and Mom used to remind us of how they had once looked.... Yea! How they had once looked... And today I stand alone on my own rubble, reminding myself, in whatever I do, of all the unimaginable cruelties they had to suffer, for nothing at all, just for being Jews! The air I breathe stands, saturated with smoke from their bodies burning in the ovens of Treblinka, Majdanek, Auschwitz and other places. The smoke drifts up to the sky in black clouds of mourning, it cries out and admonishes: "What are you people doing to another human being!" However, the air has captured the smoke and has sucked it into itself, nullifying it, not allowing it to remain as a permanent black cloud over the world. And yet, I feel the blackness of the air, being filled with that stuffy smoke that it doesn't allow itself to secrete again. The air chokes me

Page 135

and my hands fall down fainting. My feet, which have walked thousands of kilometers over all the forests, main roads and swamps, become weak. Now that I see my own home, without my loved ones, everything becomes powerless in me, my knees buckle, I have to sit down on a pile of stones of the foundation. Looking straight ahead, I discover a piece of fence, with wire on top, a remnant of the ghetto.

In shock, I close my eyes and unconsciously run my hand through the sand, digging with my fingers—I don't know what for—and feel something hard. I open my eyes and pull out an old, broken sieve. It is from our home, the potatoes were sieved with it and immediately I remember how Mom used to say with joy, "today we have a delicious meal for you children, lentils with alkalekh [potato dumplings], especially for Srolke." I cannot sit any longer and rise. My eyes drop shut, but in doing so, my gaze falls on an opening in the earth and I remember that this must be the pit I dug as a hiding place for my parents and little sister. I go and bend over it, looking for a long time into the dark opening from which a broken board peeps out; that's all I see. Heat flows through my whole body and sweat breaks out, although it is already October, autumn. The wind blows, chasing as if to flee, since it can no longer see me standing. But who can bear to come back and see something like this? I find it particularly stuffy, although everything around me is free, no house or fence cuts off my air.

I stand hunched over, peering into the darkness of the opening and can't decide, should I start digging to go in now? No! I am afraid for myself; can a man go into his own grave? Perhaps my dear parents and sister are lying there. A thought frightens me, maybe I will meet them there? How could I answer them to the question: Why have I just stopped and by what right do I come back now, treading

Page 136

on the earth soaked with their blood; and perhaps is the grass, already beginning to wilt in autumn, fertilized by the ashes of their bodies? And the soap with which I washed, from their fat? You have been torn from your lives in such an inconceivable way. Mom! Dad! Raytsele! My brothers! What should I do to justify to myself, to my own mind? Not to mention when I meet people and, pointing to myself, have to say, "I live on in this world!?" Now what resonance is there in every word about people and the world, when all at once all the affections were torn away, which one had absorbed for so many years and which meant everything that makes up a life and humanity. Stirred up by suffering, I stand there and keep looking at the opening; sit down and get up again; don't know what to do; dig up? I lack the courage. Should I go? I can't. I look around, again and again in all directions, and every glance at the surroundings makes it harder and harder for me. It begins to get dark, the evening dawns. The question occurs to me, "Where should I go now?" After all, I did come home - a winner....

It is already very dark when I leave my "home" and look around in the subsequent shattered houses, but I see neither a living person nor any other being. From a distance I notice a person walking like a shadow across the open yards. I start running, reach him and ask him in Polish: "Are there Jews living here?" He looks at me as if I am crazy and answers me: "I haven't seen any Jews at all. None here." I stop and don't know what to do anymore. I continue walking and see something bright in a window. I go into the house, a former Jewish house. A Polish woman is sitting there next to the kitchen, tinkering with something. "Dobry wieczór [Good evening!]," I say and ask her if Jews are living here. She remains lost in thought for a long time and

Page 137

answers: "They say that on Kupyitski [Kupiecka] Street some Jews have come." But she does not know for sure. I go there and actually see in front of a half-destroyed stone house with broken window panes many dirty things thrown down. On the stairs, too, a lot of different things were thrown; I go up and in the darkness of a room, sitting on a chair at a broken table, I meet a woman like a shadow, pale, haggard. It is impossible to recognize who she is. I say "gutn ovnt [good evening], voynen do idn? [are there Jews living here]?" "Yes," she answers me so quietly that I can barely hear her voice, gazing at me with a cold, dull look.

During the time when we sit there and look at each other, and, not being able to recognize our counterparts, ask each other if we are Bialystokers, her husband comes in, of whom you can see only a pair of pants and shoes dressed to a human skeleton. We talk for a long time and each inquires of the other who might have stayed? Does one of us know something about someone else, what news does he have? But how terrible it is to hear that none of us knows anything about thousands or at least hundreds of those who remained, but only about a few who can be counted on the fingers of one hand. And of the few who come later to spend the night in the apartment, after wandering the streets all day to find something edible, temporarily at old acquaintances of yore, we know only one, Dine Treshtshanksi [Dina Treszczańska], a neighbor from the past who raised me [1]. She is the only one I meet who can confirm that I am from the city. The others are all unknown to me, as if we had never lived in the same city.

Basically, we have nothing to talk about, because after all, each one of us knows everything, and yet the story seems to be different with everyone and even more cruel. In the meantime, a few more people come along, some barefoot, some without any things at all, looking for a piece of floor to lay down to sleep, all in different poses, with their fists under their heads and covered with the papers and books that are lying around in the apartment. It is hard

---

[1] *possibly it is meant that she was his nurse.*

Page 138

to suppress one's thoughts; one has to get used to them and tell oneself that this is now the reality one has been waiting for so long, enduring incredible conditions that no human imagination can ever describe; and the one who lived through it still wonders how it was actually possible to survive all that! Dine Treshtshanski [Dina Treszczańska] leads me to her room and offers me a bed; for more than a year I have not seen anything like that and I am not even used to lying in it. She beds me in clean linen, which I don't even know anymore what it looks like, and I go to sleep. I get up very late because the bed has lulled me to sleep so much. I no longer meet any of those who slept on the floor or on tables. Everyone goes around to see the former places of residence and to ask for food from acquaintances.

The First Jews Left Alive

The fight with the Nazi bandits lasts even longer; however, it is clear to all that the war will end with the victory of all united peoples fighting against fascism. On the part of the liberated Polish territory occupied by the Red Army and the fighting sections of the new Polish government, isolated Jews begin to appear, crawling out of various places, where they have lain and suffered in hiding in various ways.

Each of them is a world apart, each has persevered by different means, and yet none of them imagined that when they returned to their hometown they would encounter what they must now see with their own eyes. No one could grasp with their minds what it looked like there, and even we, who have seen it all after all, are interested in hearing from each of them again and again how they persevered.

Page 139

The first Jews from Bialystok to appear in the city immediately after the liberation were the two Okon brothers. They had been lying under the floor of a house for a year. Germans were living above them, and while the latter were stamping their feet noisily, the brothers were able to turn from one side to the other. When they ran out of prepared provisions, they ate only one jar of raw flour a day and a few raw peas for the last three months. Every day they had to reduce the portions because they did not know how long they would have to stay there. When

The historical commission in Bialystok documenting Nazi brutalities. In the center Dr. Datner, to his left Dr. Turek.

two skeletons appeared after the liberation, walking around the town and telling about themselves, nobody wanted to believe them. But the two used to ask for a jar of raw flour as proof and ate it in front of the doubters. The two were the only ones out of thousands of Jews who had been hiding [undetected]. Those who were caught were deported to Pyetrashne [Pietrasze] and, after digging pits, shot down to the smallest baby.

A 10-year-old boy of the Kovalski family remained alive. He, his

Page 140

mother and other Jews had been in hiding for many months after Bialystok was already " cleansed of Jews". But those who used to go through the streets of the ghetto to rob the remaining goods lying around discovered them in their hiding place and betrayed them to the Germans. The Germans found all the Jews, arrested them and took them by truck to Pyetrashe [Pietrasze] to be shot. Even before that, they had dug pits and ordered everyone to strip naked and go into the pits so that it would be easier for the Germans to shoot them.

It was already early evening and dark. The boy saw what was going on, hid

A group of front-line fighters and partisans at "Tsitrons at the midresh"
[Faivel Citron's Bes-Medresh] on Polne Street.

under the parked vehicles, and watched as they shot his mother and all the other Jews. In the darkness, the Germans hurried, quickly carried the [remaining] belongings to the vehicles and drove away. They did not notice the boy; he stayed there through the night and then hid until the Red Army arrived. Ten out of a hundred Jews, or, later, out of forty Jews,

Page 141

remained from those who were in the Bialystok prison. After the liquidation of the ghetto on August 16, they were put to forced labor. The General of Bialystok thought it would be a pity to kill them immediately, when he could still use their free hands to build a palace for him. However, the German law stated that there could be no more Jews in Bialystok. Thus, he ordered them to speak only Polish and to pretend to be Polish, so that he could have them work for him for free. During the day they slaved and at night they sat in prison; and whenever a few of them were no longer needed, he had them shot.

A few months before the liberation, only 40 Jews were left of them. They were forced to dig up all the places where the Germans had shot the Jews and lay the corpses on wooden boards; always a layer of people, and above that a layer of wood. After that, people and wood were doused with burning liquid and set on fire, because no traces of their continuous shootings should remain. Some [of the Jews] recognized near ones among the corpses, but had to do the work under threat of gun power, because [the Germans] were already expecting the cession of the city. When after several months of work everything was ready, they ordered [the Jews] to dig a pit and strip naked; and 30 armed Germans were waiting with their rifles to shoot them. However, the Jews saw what was going on, rushed at the Germans naked or half-naked and with their bare hands, made their way through and ran apart. 30 Jews fell, 10 managed to get to safety and hid in the city for the last few weeks waiting for liberation.

Apart from the partisans who, on their own initiative, took their fate into their own hands from the first minute, understanding that the struggle is the only way to liberation, individual Jews, who can be counted on the fingers of one hand, returned in unbelievable, various ways.. The smallest resistance,

Page 142

even that with bare hands, as the case with the 40 Jews, offered more security to stay alive than remaining in despondency or clinging to a religious point of view, when in some cases it was said that this [catastrophe] was a "gzar" [judgment of God or decree]. Life is absolutely no "gzar", and with hope and faith in one's own strength, which one must always muster in moments of relapse, one can save oneself. Each [of these] battles is a battle won, and if not for all who fight, then definitely for those who learn from it. However, if you take the path of despondency in conjunction with "advocates or mediators," you are lost; and for those who have learned this path and want to continue on it, all is lost. We, all surviving Jews, had to learn this lesson, and so we turn to our brethren, who demand of us an answer to the question, "What happened?" "This has happened!" we reply to them. And no matter how bluntly we talk and how awful our never-healing wounds are: The fact that people wanted to save their own lives by selling the others, that they put their own egos above the welfare of their whole people and our one hundred percent annihilation, is merely a product of governance.

The small parts of the Jewish youth who were educated in the revolutionary spirit, constantly fighting against the other types of leaderships and education, proved, before the whole world and for the future, that even in the cruelest times of our people, those of us survived only thanks to active resistance. After all, the 20 percent who fell died a dignified death, like all the peoples' fighters, on an equal footing with everyone, because in these conditions people perishing in battle is inevitable.

Yom Kippur in Bialystok, 1944

Any Jew who remembers Yom Kippur, related to what he saw and witnessed at home in his town or city,

Page 143

will have deep memories regardless of his view or attitude toward the religious ceremony. With trepidation in his heart, he will remember being young and at home with his parents on that special day, which was for all different than any other day of the year. [Just to mention] the emptiness in the streets, the crowded synagogues and especially, the mood of the people in the synagogues. However, I remember the Yom Kippur in Bialystok of 1944, when out of 60,000 Jews barely thirty Jews gathered, in addition to ten persons coming from the province. I have to focus specifically on that day on the question of what actually brought us to the synagogue at that time, not only us, but also the Jewish officers of the Red Army, who were supposed to stand there with a "sider" [Jewish prayer book] in their hands and pray, or those Jewish officers of the new Polish Army who were supposed to do the same. Above all, however, [I remember] a Jew with a cross on his chest, who came back to the Jews, and of whom it was not ascertainable what he, silently, wanted to do with the cross, and to whom he was actually praying.

Nature has its own course, as it did thousands of years ago, and it is not particularly interested in what is happening on man's earth and what changes man is making in their economic-political sphere. It does not make a fuss about it. Autumn is approaching in our region, with its fierce, cold winds and rains, where it is already necessary to prepare the winter laundry and seal the windows against the rain pouring in. My apartment at that time was on Kupyitski [Kupiecka] Street 39, in an old, ruined building with broken windows. It was a half, dark, sooty room with wallpaper torn on all sides, without electricity, with only a rag as a wick in a small bottle, an empty bed without a blanket, a broken table with three and a half legs found somewhere, which often fell over when I leaned on it or a comrade did not pay attention and leaned on it. So the few of us who have remained alive are sitting there right now, telling each other various episodes of our former lives, memories, when someone speaks up: "Come, let's find out where the Kol Nidre is prayed!" No need to pray for a long time. Nothing is there to go to or do anyway.

Page 144

It is cold in the room, everything is open. Today you don't have to walk long through streets and alleys, as you once did, because as soon as you come out, you walk right across the courtyards, streets, houses, everything has been razed to the ground. In the past, if you wanted to go to the Mlynove [Młynowa] Street 157 to pray, as we do today, you had to turn through alleys and streets, but today it is a pleasure: "freedom and equality", [so to speak], because the roads are free of houses and, as far as equality is concerned, everything is level with the earth.

Approaching in the darkness, we see from afar that something is shining in a window of a new house; we go inside and immediately see the following at first glance: In the eastern corner of a small room there is a table with lighted candles; the whole room is full of Jews, most of them are men and maybe six women, nothing more. All standing together and crying, all with hairy faces and in old, torn clothes. So each of them stand, facing their wounds. Not a single Jew without a beard, not a single child. All between the ages of 25 and 45, plus military men, officers from all armies, common soldiers or those with decorations, some invalids. The one at the omed [podium] is davening, but you can barely hear him, because from every angle and side another "oy!" rings out with a sigh and chokes in convulsions. Without prayer shawls, without white robes, but with big wounds in their hearts and swollen eyes, they stand there close together, but where are the thoughts and looks of each of them turned to?! I can't tell, because I can't read their minds; they are very different Jews: There is that tall Russian officer standing by, holding a Jewish prayer book next to his chest full of medals, and crying. I wonder if he is praying seriously. One cannot believe it! After all, only one thing I do believe, concluding from me to others: After losing everyone during the war and facing the reality, which proved to be cruel, many hopes that were placed in people while they were at the front, ready to sacrifice their lives, proved to be deceptive, and they became shaken [in their values and faith]. Looking for

Page 145

a place where they could get everything off their chest, they came to the synagogue to sob their heart out.

How difficult it is for those who had to go through all this to answer all the questions! There' s a Jew pretending to be a Pole. A big mustache, a Polish hat, appropriate boots and a cross on his chest. Hard to tell if he is a Jew or not, but his eyes are puffy. He's not holding a prayer book, just a cane. I look at him and try to get an idea of this person, according to his posture and behavior, "what is he doing?" He seems broken; what kind of hell of human suffering has he gone through?! Since he may not have been so religious before, he may have converted from the Jewish faith and now, in the silence, when all eyes are watching him, he cries along with everyone, responds with "omeyn!", does not take down the cross, but is interested in all Jewish content. Afterwards, I actually learned that this Jew later lost his life in a raid by Poles on a shtetl to which 10 Jews had returned. He died while he was in the shtetl among Jews; that's how his life ended. After all, on Yom Kippur, everyone had gone to the synagogue specifically to come clean with themselves, not to ask someone else's forgiveness and wish them a good year, but to demand a response, from God, from others, or from themselves. Not to "knock Al-Khet" [say the prayer of repentance] they came, but to "knock the table" ["clear the air"]; not to say a prayer for the deceased, but to obtain satisfaction for their souls and for themselves, to find an answer to all that had happened.

It was not the prayer ceremony of those days, where occasionally you could even hear the words of the khazn [cantor] standing on the podium and performing all his duties in terms of reciting the prayers. Rarely did anyone care about the [individual] words of the prayers they heard from the khazn. However, what was said then, connected man with his people, and the momentary broad connection, no matter what class or stratum a person belonged to and what views he held, so tore the individual apart that he was drawn into the small

Page 146

courtyard and into the dark room to find something that would give him relief and answer his questions. After all, when we finally left the prayer ceremony, our thoughts became even more bitter and somber as we realized what we had become and what we looked like now, after the expected victory.

The First Step to a New Life

Just as the millennia-old Jewish legend tells of the time when the Flood subsided and Noah let out a pair of each kind of living creature so that it could develop again in the world after its kind, so now the first Jews are coming together. Each one of different stratum goes back now to his former work: a shoemaker, a manufacturer, a turner, from each fellow-one. Each in his own way creates a workshop and begins to work.

In the evening we all meet and discuss about the conditions of our new life, that one person succeeds better in integrating and the second worse. The "stronger" one already hires the newcomer, who is not yet coping well with the new situation and pays him a fixed wage per working day. Life makes its own demands, not knowing anything about brokenness and sentimentalities. You live? —Then continue to fight for your life and prepare your way according to the laws in which you find yourself. The first committee arises from itself; it is not elected. Those who are interested take the work into their own hands. Every evening, also a small number of pious Jews sit together and study the Gemara. Once I was very impressed by the scene I saw there. When I happened to come into the room where the committee used to meet during the day, I met ten young Jews sitting and studying old religious book pages that had been gathered together. I stood

Page 147

there for maybe ten minutes thinking how people at a time like this could sit with so much patience and a clear head; young people who had endured so much were learning topics that were written so many years ago and even still discussed them, just as if everything had gone normally, as if nothing had happened.

The answer to the above can be found in the tendency to cling to the "old" even when it is doomed. But now, after all our people have been handed over

Back to life: Bialystok schoolchildren with their teachers

to mass murder without distinction, we as a whole must face the struggle against the old system that is killing us, and fight to continue to exist as a people. In every struggle that took place in the world, our people used to find a way in the currents that brought the new ideas and developed them, and in the present struggle between the old world system and the new concepts to be realized, our way is to support the new and fight for

Page 148

a system that contains the call for love between people and against mutual exploitation. For the old system, with its racial hatred and exploitation of peoples, is firmly rooted and demands to remain.

My intention is not that the reader groans or regrets the fate of the people who were in the middle of the events and had to go through such cruel experiences, but that he should form a judgment according to the facts I mention and the pictures I have seen, because I have experienced everything myself, in my own body. [My book] should be understood as a call to reconsider the existing attitudes and ideas and not to lift hands for continuing to bring to power those people who stand for the same old system, but to go into resistance against them with all means. In this way we can pay tribute and honor the memory of all the fallen and loved ones, our parents, brothers, sisters, wives, children, grandfathers and grandmothers, the innocently murdered and the fighters in the armies and partisan groups in the ghetto.

End Page

Preparation of this book for publication
was completed 24 May 1947
at the OPTIMUS Graphic Studios
2719 V. Gómez Street
Buenos Aires

APPENDIX

Epilogue

(provided by Srolke Kot's family)

After the second world war ended, Srolke Kot decided to live in Palestine. He settled in Haifa, taking a ship from the Italian port of Bari, a ship which he often thought was about to sink into the Mediterranean. While in Haifa, his sole surviving brother, Meyer Kot, who had left for Argentina before the war, managed to find him and they began corresponding. Srolke's letters to Meyer about his experiences during the Holocaust became the seeds of this book, and were published in the Yiddish newspaper in Buenos Aires.

In 1947 Meyer succeeded in bringing Srolke to Argentina. He had to enter with a false passport via Paraguay as the government at the time did not allow him to migrate legally.

Once in Argentina, Srolke settled into a new life with the help of his brother, always maintaining his links to his fellow countrymen from Bialystok and other survivors of the Holocaust. He met and married Helena Zimmerspitz, an Argentina-born daughter of a Poland-born father and Russia-born mother, with whom he had and raised two daughters. Helena passed away in 1983.

Srolke (or Zeide, as he was called by his family) integrated into Argentinian society, applying himself to commerce. He and his wife had a grocery store and later he sold children's clothing. He participated in various community committees, such as for a banking cooperative. He continued writing throughout his life, including a column on current affairs and politics in his local newspaper which ran for many years.

He dedicated a large part of his life to anti-fascism and the telling of his story and that of the suffering of the Jews in World War Two. This included giving numerous talks at events commemorating ghetto uprisings and the Holocaust more generally and volunteering his time at the Buenos Aires Shoah Museum.

Despite his horrific experiences, Srolke lived with great joy and humour. Through his life and writing he taught all those who got to know him of the importance of the struggle against injustice and to never give up. For that we are truly grateful.

Srolke passed away in 2007 at the age of 90. He is survived by two daughters, three grandchildren and six great-grandchildren. The eldest of his great-grandchildren honours his memory by having Srolke as his middle name.

Srolke Kot

Wedding photo of Srolke and Helena Zimmerspitz, 1953

List of Names/ **Khurbn Bialystok**

Aberzinski	85
Afronasitsh	72
Andreyev, commander	120
Barash, engineer	36, 38, 55, 58, 81
Borov(n)ik, Shepsl	97, 108, 109
Datner, Dr. Shimon	75, 101, 114, 115, 139
Donskoy	80
Epshteyn	27
Farber	45, 96
Feyge Bayle	26
Filipov, commander	121,126
Fin	35
Fishl	78
Friedel	47, 49
Genye	26
Goldberg	36
Grosman, Khaye	89
Groza	73
Karpovitsh	96
Khalef [or Khalif], Khayim	79, 104, 117, 112, 113
Khaye the Grober's son	27
KhayimVelvel,	26
Khilek	95
Khlavne	26
Kirzhner, Nyome [Kole]	109
Kot, Leybl [Beybe]	11, 23, 28, 29, 42, 45, 58, 60, 61, 63, 70, 76, 77, 78, 82,84
Kot, Nyome	11, 22, 27, 28, 40, 41
Kot, Raytsele	37, 41, 42, 51, 52, 61, 66, 77, 78, 136
Kot, Srolke	Author
Kovalski family	139
Kvater	35
Love [Lowe], Simkhe	96
Madeyska, Rivke	91
Malmed	67
Marek	98, 99
Markus	59
Moti	58, 62,
Motl Tshremoshne	110
Nowogrodzka, Judith	72
Okon brothers	139
Roz[en]man, the Rabbi	25, 36

Printed in the USA
CPSIA information can be obtained
at www.ICGtesting.com
LVHW011528280923
759191LV00001B/2